REMOTE
LEADERSHIP

www.amplifypublishing.com

Remote Leadership:

How to Accelerate Achievement and Create a Community in a Work-from-Home World

For more information, please contact:

Amplify Publishing, an imprint of Mascot Books

620 Herndon Parkway, Suite 320

Herndon, VA 20170

info@amplifypublishing.com

Library of Congress Control Number: 2021912882

CPSIA Code: PRFRE0821A

ISBN-13: 978-1-64543-539-6

Printed in Canada

REMOTE

David
Pachter

LEADERSHIP

How to Accelerate Achievement
and Create a Community
in a Work-from-Home World

amplify

CONTENTS

FOREWORD
Leading from Afar

Here's an unsurprising observation: business schools don't teach would-be leaders how to manage during a pandemic. Indeed, most common sense and useful leadership truisms need to be reexamined, rethought, and ultimately updated to work in a world where "work" is more of a verb than a noun.

Take my son's job as an example. A recent graduate of a design program focused on user experience and interaction, he landed a job (in the middle of the COVID-19 pandemic) after never having met in person the people with whom he would work nor the manager to whom he would report. The company, a startup based in San Diego, offered a great opportunity for someone with little experience. He moved from New York for the job—to San Francisco because the San Diego office remains closed. This past winter, itching to get out, he and two friends—remote workers themselves—decamped for

Mexico for a month. He left on a Friday, surfed on a Saturday, and was back to "work" on Sunday—logged into Slack, running through designs for a facelift to the mobile version of the company's app and in time for a Zoom-based presentation to the CEO of the findings of a usability study. Then he went fishing and caught a barracuda. Breaded and deep-fried barracuda, he assured me, is delicious.

When I was a young man first learning how to lead both through trial and error (or trial by fire), the brilliant leadership teacher Tom Peters was popularizing one of the significant principles taught at one of the most successful companies of the late twentieth century: Hewlett-Packard. First coined at HP but made widely popular by Peters was the notion of management by wandering around, or MBWA.

As Peters taught, MBWA is a metaphor for being in touch, for not losing touch with customers, contractors, and—most importantly—employees and colleagues. Peters stresses that this discipline—the discipline of getting out from behind a desk, getting out of your office, and getting close to the people who are actually conducting the day-to-day of your organization's defining work—is one key factor in the search for excellence that drives most leaders. MBWA, taught Peters, allows the leader to know their customers and their employees and colleagues and to feel—really feel—the challenges, struggles, and opportunities of the business. It is a way of getting beyond static reports and the very real human tendency to hide the bad and promote the good. It is a way of cutting through the naturally arising delusions that too often pass for management directives. It's a way of getting to the truth of your organization.

So how do you do these things when you have employees on a beach in Mexico, in a one-bedroom apartment in San Diego, or in their childhood bedroom at home with their parents? Peters, as well as the other giants of leadership development, never expected a virus to send us out of our office and into our homes, permanently changing the way we work. Indeed, those who wrote the textbooks on leading never envisioned that all of their work would have to be translated and updated for a world in which "wandering around" means by video with hundreds, if not thousands, of miles, and three or four time zones separating teammates.

We could, of course, see this situation as temporary. Once the pandemic has ended, we'll all roll back to things as they were. But we would be delusional. The trend to remote work, like trends toward online (or "remote") shopping and learning, began long before 2020. The pandemic accelerated the trend, and employees such as my son are never going to go back to a daily commute, stale office coffee, and in-person only "all team" meetings.

This new reality demands that *management by walking around* be replaced by *leading from afar*.

David Pachter enters this disrupted world and offers simple but powerful evidence and experienced-based guidance for leading in a work-from-home world. Gathered long before the pandemic but coalesced during the worst of the time apart, *Remote Leadership* shows us the ways the remote, and generally asynchronous, workplace is now longer determined by *place*.

With place being anywhere, he notes, "the coercive organization is dead." Coercive leadership is replaced by reflective leadership in which the leaders "naturally possess the self-awareness to understand and accept their weaknesses, the ability to see themselves as others do, and the metacognition to manage their thoughts, feelings, and responses in real time."

"Our ability to see others is a critical part of leading," he writes, "but it is based on our ability to see ourselves."

The conclusion, therefore, is clear: to lead well, to really see—or as Tom Peters would argue, to be in touch with our colleagues and our customers—requires that we see ourselves clearly. Leading from afar, then, places a heightened demand on the leader's ability to cut through their own delusions. The Mexico-based, surfing, barracuda-eating UI experts who are building our companies demand their leaders cut through, tell the truth, and build trust.

For when our employees can't touch us, can't see us, hear us, sense us, can't know us, how can they trust us? And when we can't see and know them, how can we trust them?

In my work as a writer, a coach, and a CEO, I teach a concept called radical self-inquiry by asking leaders and others who hold power, "How have you been complicit in creating the conditions you *say* you don't want?" Such self-inquiry cuts through the masks we learned to wear and strips away delusions such as "It's *always* the other person's fault."

Well executed, such radically reflective leadership—shared with guts and vulnerability—creates a trust bond that enables all in the organization to know that while I'm doing my work here, you will do your work there.

It's tempting to lament the pandemic-induced flight to work-from-home. And it's true that no silver lining will ever bring back those lost or heal the wounds and devastation their deaths inflicted on each of us. But we can extract lessons from these times?

One poignant lesson I took from this accelerated movement toward a distributed and asynchronous world is how much we actually need each other. In dozens of talks with thousands of employees, I bore witness to their suffering. I've encouraged leaders to forego quick and easy fixes to the problems of their colleagues' lives.

I've watched relief (and, more often than not, tears) flood employees' faces as we spoke of the face mask not as a political ideal but as a symbol of our interconnectedness. "I need you to wear a mask," I told a gathering of employees who'd logged into a video call from Mumbai, Nairobi, New York, and San Francisco, "as you need me to wear a mask." That is how viruses work.

I told them that is one way we stay connected and in touch.

Over the course of the months as uncertainty and turmoil caused us to redefine the workplace (and, in doing so, work itself), another need became even more clear: the need for an in touch and shared sense of purpose.

There was a reason why when I shared a teaching from my Buddhist teacher, Pema Chodron, folks would cry. The teaching, that our task in the midst of the storm of uncertainty, is to sit like a "mountain in a hurricane," caused folks to cry because they saw it in a path. Moreover, as we would speak to this notion—the mountain in a hurricane of uncertainty and disruption, of change and reinvention—we inevitably hit upon the thing that is unchanging, even after our employees and colleagues have scattered across the world. That is our shared sense of purpose.

We may no longer be able to walk around, stand over a colleague's desk, ask after their parents' health or their kindergartener's recital, but touch into purpose. Purpose, mission, and values still bind us— no matter how far apart we may be.

While up to now, business schools may not have been teaching about remote leadership, that will change. It has to. Our old ways have been disrupted forever and, with the benefit of a bit of distance, we know, for the better.

Jerry Colonna
CEO and cofounder of Reboot.io and author of
Reboot: Leadership and the Art of Growing Up

INTRODUCTION

I never liked the idea of people working from home. I wanted them to be in the office, accountable for meeting their key performance indicators (KPIs) and feeding off each other's energy. By early 2019, that philosophy seemed to be working out just fine. JumpCrew, the company I cofounded in 2016 to offer outsourced sales and marketing services to brands like Twitter and Alibaba, had just gone on a growth binge.

In Q4 of 2018, we'd hired one hundred people in one hundred days. We'd gone from a headcount of thirty to about two hundred and fifty in what seemed like the blink of an eye, and our Nashville offices were hopping with activity and enthusiasm. I saw no reason why 2019 and 2020 couldn't hold more of the same.

Scottish poet Robert Burns wrote, "The best-laid schemes o' mice an' men often go awry." Damn you, Bobby. Along came March of 2020, when the World Health Organization declared the spread of the novel coronavirus to be a pandemic, and it became clear that businesses everywhere, including JumpCrew, would need to shut down their offices and send everyone home, where they would work remotely via laptop and desktop computers, Zoom and Google Meet, Slack, and their smart phones.

So in just a few weeks, the young, busy, aggressive company we'd spent four years building furloughed one hundred people and rewrote its leadership playbook. We turned off the lights and told everybody to get comfortable in their home offices, because once the team was all settled in with their Wi-Fi and their webcams, it was back to business. JumpCrew has always had an accelerated, achievement-based culture, and we had no intention of letting COVID-19 change that.

If only we had been as confident as that sounded. Truthfully, we didn't know what work from home (WFH) meant for our company. We had no idea what would happen when we went fully remote— when managers weren't there to look over people's shoulders, when customers had to compete for attention with fidgety preschoolers and yellow Labs begging for walks, when employees were isolated and anxious instead of telling jokes in the break room. Nobody did. At the same time, many of our earlier stage clients found themselves desperate in unsustainable businesses. Spring 2020 marked the beginning of an unplanned global experiment in corporate adaptability.

Rob, my partner and JumpCrew's CEO, has called the COVID-19 pandemic an accelerant for change, and he's right. Before March of 2020, WFH was an idea every organization, large and small, had discussed but few had implemented at scale. LinkedIn research from 2019 showed that almost half of professionals were working from home at least one day per week, and 82 percent of working professionals said they would like to work from home one day a week or more, with 57 percent wanting to work from home three or more days a week. However, WFH was never the game changer everyone expected it to be. According to the Bureau of Labor Statistics, from 2017–2018, only about 28 percent of full-time employees worked from home at least some of the time.[1]

Why did the reality of WFH historically fall short of its potential? Lots of reasons, but I think there were two main reasons for the resistance to WFH. First, there were few successful models for building and practically operating a company where the entire workforce was remote. Second was the traditional notion of command-and-control authority commonly associated with leadership. Most executive leaders still believe they are expected to solve all problems and create an undercurrent of urgency by pacing the halls and sticking their heads into offices and cubicles—what Tom Peters and Robert H. Waterman called "management by walking around" in their book *In Search of Excellence*. Plus, most leaders assume that working from home equals *not working*, which is what I used to think.

Now, because of the eat-your-vegetables moment forced on us by the pandemic, this more self-absorbed leadership paradigm may be on its way out and not a moment too soon. Driven by pragmatic necessity and survival instinct, WFH experienced an unprecedented boom in 2020. According to the *2020 Global Work-From-Home Experience Survey* created by Isometrics, 88 percent of all office workers around the world worked from home more than one day per week during the pandemic—including an amazing *97 percent* of office workers in North America—compared with just 31 percent pre-pandemic.[2]

What's just as incredible is how happy WFH workers were back when the survey was conducted:

- Seventy-three percent said they were very successful working from home.
- Eighty-six percent in North America said they felt fully productive at home.
- Eighty-two percent in the U.S. said they wanted to continue working from home after COVID-19 at least part of the time.
- Seventy percent of managers reported being just as satisfied or more satisfied with employee performance in WFH as they were when everyone was in the office.

WFH became *the* business success story of the pandemic. Remote worker support company Lifehack even launched the online tool remote.lifeshack.io to help users track the WFH policies of hundreds of companies, from Amazon to Zillow. So workers are happy, managers are happy, and presumably, stockholders are happy. This WFH thing is a breeze, right?

Not so fast. Polling for the *2020 Global Work-From-Home Experience Survey* was conducted in March and April of 2020, when working from one's spare bedroom was still new and exciting. The peak seemed to be in early May, when a Gallup poll[3] found that 52 percent of U.S. workers said they were working from home 100 percent of the time. But as spring turned into summer, the WFH honeymoon seemed to come to an end.

The *New York Times* and NPR published pieces with titles like "The Long, Unhappy History of Working from Home" and "Why Remote Work Sucks, According To Science." *Pitchbook* published a doom-and-gloom piece[4] about how the flight of "tech pros" from the virus was gutting entrepreneurial hubs like San Francisco and Silicon Valley. A Monster.com survey[5] conducted in July 2020 found that 69 percent of remote workers were experiencing symptoms of burnout—up 18 percent from just two months earlier.

The takeaway: *WFH isn't a panacea.* Yes, some people and companies have flourished in it. Many organizations will probably continue WFH in some form—a few days in the office, a few days at home—when the pandemic is in the rearview mirror. But for some employees, it's gotten old. They feel isolated, cut off from friends, and stuck in a loop where there's no end to the workday. Even managers and senior executives feel cut off from their people and have been working longer hours, both because of their own lack of clear boundaries and the constant drumbeat of problems that need fixing.

Of course, there have been sudden, seismic shifts in the meaning and execution of leadership before. What leadership looks like and the expectations of the behavior of leaders is changing all the time, and 2020 presented multiple opportunities to demonstrate growth and progress in the shadow of other circumstances. While the COVID pandemic forced leaders to reimagine WFH, the voices for change surrounding Black Lives Matter compelled many leaders to address issues related to racism and the need for diversity within their organizations at the same time. The point is leadership is always changing in the face of events large and small and will do so again. These principles will apply when leading in WFH seems as routine and normal as making breakfast or walking to the corner store.

Today, WFH isn't an emergency anymore. It's the new normal, and we're over it. But it's here to stay, so we've got to find a way to make it work. The key, as with most things in business, turns out to be effective leadership.

Disruption Becomes Mission

COVID meant that JumpCrew's smaller clients suffered the most. Client churn went sky high, and our cash flow was terrible. We adapted quicky and are now thriving again as an organization and as individuals. The team rallied around the crisis as we furloughed some people and implemented pay cuts, and by the end of 2020, our revenues had surpassed pre-COVID levels. We are hiring dozens of new people each month, and morale has never been higher.

WFH has been a success story for JumpCrew, and I say that as the guy who not long ago was opposed to anybody working from home. But it's not just that we've done well in the WFH world. Many companies have done that. It's *why* we've done so well that matters. It's not because of our technology or training or because we threw millions of dollars at the problem. It's because by the time the world changed, we had already built a culture that prepared our leaders to spearhead that change in a way that was mindful, connected, vulnerable, and transparent while holding our people accountable for meeting sky-high expectations. That's why I wrote this book.

We managed the transition from office to home with our hair on fire while trying to appear calm. The virus was a week or two later in coming to Nashville than it was to New York, but a lot of our hires had come from New York. People were scared, and we knew we had to shut down quickly. In early March, about a week before Nashville had its mandatory shutdowns, we closed our doors.

During that transition period, JumpCrew leadership was communicating continuously with everyone from senior managers to new hires, managing expectations, and letting all employees know that everyone would be patient and understanding during this tumultuous time. Then we held our breath and waited to see if our little sales organization, which had always fed off the kind of in-person, fist-bumping electricity that's typical in sales bullpens, would survive without that energy source.

The results exceeded our wildest expectations. To be fair, some of that was because we weren't a startup anymore, and the investments we made in our culture, training, and process were substantial. A lot of the applause also goes to our people, some of whom had been asking for the freedom to work from home and who now faced a "put up or shut up" moment. Well, they really put up. Accountability is a huge part of what we call our "accelerated achievement" culture, and everyone knew that after a short adjustment period, they would be expected to adapt and keep hitting their KPIs without a lot of hand-holding. Our team, like many others, embraced the sense of mission that came with the big shift to working from home and delivered.

But the real difference maker was the community and connection that we had started building long before COVID-19. In an environment where people have no personal contact, where there is no break room to chat about the Titans game or after-work happy hour to build camaraderie, you might expect a company's culture to degrade as everyone retreats into their own little world. But Jump-Crew's culture has actually gotten *stronger*, and I attribute that to three strategies that we brought in early on—strategies that have made us a better, more resilient organization.

The Great Remote Organization

Writing for the *MIT Sloan Management Review*, Alec Levenson and Patrick McLaughlin wrote of the COVID-19 world, "Some organizations are pivoting hard to new delivery channels, new products, and new operating models without having enough time to manage the impact of these changes thoughtfully. As a result, many executives currently find themselves shooting from the hip, bereft of their usual channels to engage deeply with stakeholders and gain agreement on the path forward . . . More than ever, leaders must be attuned to the needs of their businesses and their people, even though the stresses in their own lives may have increased during the pandemic."[6]

Post-COVID, it won't matter whether an organization adopts a full-WFH business model or a hybrid model with employees balancing in-office and remote work. Leaders will confront the harsh reality that the top-down, autocratic leadership approach of figures like Martha Stewart is irrelevant in the WFH world. Many are confronting it already.

Let's face it, a lot of the activities that define traditional "leading"—impromptu "do it this way" mentoring; sidebar chats in the halls; the intimidation factor of the boss watching and listening, dominating meetings, and riding to the rescue when a client failure or disagreement brings progress to a halt—rely on everybody being physically present. In the office, executives can easily engage with subordinates and steer the ship without being too intentional about what they're doing and why.

That's gone. In its place is a distributed working world where leaders who aspire to build strong remote organizations don't just need new skills but new *philosophies*. In your remote enterprise, each employee is in his or her own world, a single-serving CEO of themselves. Your team can't draw energy from random encounters or bond over birthday cake. When your group is on the edge of fracturing, leadership-based sharing, communication, self-awareness, vulnerability, compassion, and humility is what holds it together and leads to a tribal bond, a culture of personal growth, and a universal desire to achieve exceptional results.

That's an organization becoming a community. It's what Jump-Crew was long before COVID-19. If you want to grow a distributed business in an age when WFH is no longer a heart-pumping five-alarm emergency but the new ordinary, you'll need to know how to build community, culture, and connection in the same way.

- To hire brilliantly and fire with both compassion and speed.
- To lead with an apology and ask better questions.
- To own your shortcomings and work to become the best leader you can be.
- To stop talking and really listen.
- To lean into the hard conversations when they need to be had.
- To be a coach who enables your team to lead you.
- To be a little bit Buddhist and a little bit rock and roll.

In this book, I'll share the Three Pillars of great remote organizations:

Reflective Leadership. You're committed to doing the work. To see yourself as others do, think before you act, align your actions with your words, and look back before you go forward. Reflective leaders are aware of the messages their behavior sends, are in search of self-defeating programs that compel them to make the same poor decisions, and are focused on acting mindfully. Reflective leadership is about knowing yourself, accepting your fallibility, and working to improve. Because they're free from having to be the source of all knowledge and courage, reflective leaders find peace, confidence, and self-compassion and eliminate the parts of their mental program that cause conflict.

Coaching Mindset and Culture. In a coaching-centric organization, the leader's primary job is no longer to give advice and solve problems. It's to release control, encourage self-exploration in others, and share experiences that help employees find their own solutions. Ego gratification does not come from being the Big Man (or Woman) on Campus but from helping the people you mentor and guide find their own best self. Great coaches ask great questions, take risks, and build on what exists. They are also learners who learn to coach themselves. You don't find the sage at the bottom of the mountain.

Peer Learning. Peer learning is about creating trust in groups and enabling deeper conversations between people across the organization who might not ever meet. The learning happens in small group forums (for us, carried out remotely on the Circl.es platform). It gives individual contributors a safe space to be themselves, practice openness, forge meaningful relationships, cultivate respect, and become resources for one another's growth, all without the mediation of a boss. Norms or the rules of engagement—commit, contribute, and confide—guide more personal conversations and create a safe space that encourages exploration of what's true rather than what confirms their biases. Participants commit to not giving advice. Instead, peer learning groups share personal experiences.

> Listening to other people's experiences is nonthreatening and nonjudgmental. When we hear a story, we take what is useful to us. The best advice is personal: wisdom drawn from our experience, not solely our judgments or instincts. When that advice is delivered in the form of a great story, it's more likely to be heard and remembered. Your ability

to share a similar experience fosters a culture of agency and autonomy.

On the other hand, when I give advice I'm making it about me—"You know what, Marc, I think you should follow up with the prospect in one week"—Marc is not as likely to feel responsible for what comes of that action and choice. If it blows up in his face, he'll be more likely to come back to me with "Thanks a lot, David, I did what you told me, and it was a disaster." Advice inhibits growth and accountability, minimizes empowerment, and erodes trust when the advice isn't taken or the result isn't positive. Experience sharing is about investing in someone else's success. Advice can come from the same place—a good place—but gently redirecting it into experience sharing honors the other person and fuels continued focus, curiosity, and trust.

For generations, business has been about the people at the top. The cult of the CEO. The celebrities in the C-suite. But those companies are not as resilient. Individual contributors don't care about the organization because the organization doesn't care about them, so turnover is high, loyalty and engagement are low, and when there's a crisis—say, a pandemic—few give extra effort because the relationship between leaders and individual contributors is transactional: *Do your job, and I won't fire you.*

When Rob called to ask me if I'd partner with him and start JumpCrew, he was almost two years into trying to change the culture in the sales organization that acquired our prior company. He led by saying, "I'm done busting my ass to try and fix someone else's broken shit." We had a great culture at our last startup, so he knew I'd know what he was talking about. Before he could close by threatening to start a new venture with or without me, I knew I was in. In imagining JumpCrew, we set out to give employees the support they needed to ramp up quickly and leverage every bit of their innate talent and passion while quickly spotting the people who didn't fit and letting them go fast.

That meant the company couldn't be about us. JumpCrew had to be about our people, about giving them what they needed to create a community built on a shared vision and respect, the aspiration to be great, hold each other accountable, and show up as their best selves every day, WFH or not.

Of course, everything flows downstream from leadership, so this fresh approach to culture had to start with us. We had to be reflective and face our own demons. We had to quit saying, "Do it this way" and start asking, "What do you think a good solution would be?" We had to get out of the way so our people could learn from one another. You know what we discovered? It turns out that's exactly the approach you need to successfully lead a distributed organization in a WFH world.

What I'll Share

I'm going to show you why the Three Pillars are the keys to accelerating achievement and building community in this strange new normal. As we found out, creating a community that makes people feel heard and seen encourages leaders to be vulnerable and empowers teams to be their own sources of energy. It is one hell of an operating system for making a remote organization that runs smoothly and grows steadily.

When everyone scattered to their homes, we had already created the connections where people felt trusted and empowered to do the best work of their lives. Our team felt connected to one another and to us, even though we couldn't physically connect on the spur of the moment. Turnover dropped, and while some of that was surely due to the recession, we were also soon to be rehiring like crazy. By December 2020, 30 percent of the company were post-WFH hires. WFH also dramatically expanded our hiring pool. Before, we had been recruiting the best of Nashville; now we were recruiting from a pool of the best and brightest all over the United States.

Those results were incredibly validating. I had been working on the ideas that led to this book for years. I started with a pure focus on individual achievement that I called JumpbyDesign. It was my own story of finding the focus and discipline needed to achieve, and it never felt like the whole story. I had reinvented myself from prep school slacker to Hollywood movie producer. Then from humbled salesman to startup CEO (enjoying a couple of good exits) to burnout case by forty-five years old. I struggled through the effects of my wife's death from cancer and my young daughter's long illness, and at the same time, my startup was on life support. I was always on in one way or another.

I hadn't seen a therapist in years until the day my wife entered hospice. On that day, my friend Doug called and offered me his session. I didn't know his therapist, but it seemed like a generous and timely gift, and I accepted it. What started as crisis counseling became a journey in self-reflection that changed the way I see myself, my relationships, and the world. I formed a bond with the therapist and set about the journey of doing the work to see my own behavior more clearly and examine the decisions I was making that had become counterproductive "programs." Over time, I recognized how my own communication skill (or lack thereof) was limiting my relationships and my ability to live a more satisfying and fulfilling life. That commitment to doing the work made this book possible, and that journey is still going on. I live it daily.

One thing I found is that when you surrender to achievement, you also surrender control of your time. Maniacal focus can be addictive, and it's counterintuitive to think about doing less to achieve more. So while reflective leadership is all about discovering radical self-inquiry as a secret of true success, I never understood that until I finally took a badly needed sabbatical and washed up in Barcelona, where I fell in with a like-minded fraternity of seekers and sages, including people you'll hear from later in this book. That experience inspired me to dig deeper and do more of the personal heavy lifting that became the heart of *Remote Leadership*.

The story I had been telling myself about WFH companies was, "People work from home when they don't want to work." I knew that if someone had given me the opportunity to work from home at twenty-six years old, I'd have spent most of the day playing basketball. I saw that behind my own anti-WFH bias was existential fear—the fear that if people worked from home, they would slack off, the company would go under, and I would be humiliated. The pandemic forced me to face that fear, a fear that many founders and CEOs—and maybe even you—share.

In these pages, I'll share the inner workings of the Three Pillars, my insights into how to implement them, hiring strategies for a remote organization—everything you need to build and lead a winning remote organization in a world where the old benchmarks of leadership no longer make sense. But I'm going to go beyond that because WFH offers something else: a way to be a leader without it costing you *everything*.

We've all seen the price some entrepreneurs and senior executives pay for success, from poor physical and mental health to damaged family relationships. But while WFH is redefining what it means to operate a business, it's also giving us the chance to rewrite what success looks like. When you don't have to be first in the office, when you don't have to solve all the problems, when you can be flawed and vulnerable and come to a meeting in your sweatpants, what does that mean? Can leading successfully be about doing less? Taking time for yourself? Being a better parent, spouse, neighbor, and human? We'll dig deep into those questions and find some answers.

I'll share how you can build a high-performing organization based on deeper relationships, a sense of community, self-acceptance, courageous questioning, and mutual accountability. A place where you won't need to have all the answers so you can ask better questions. You won't teach; you'll share. You won't give orders; you'll bring out the best in others while trusting them to guide themselves, each other, and sometimes you. If you've not yet done really hard things well in your career, I'm going to help you get closer by doing a bunch of small things well.

Let's get started.

David Pachter
Somewhere in New York
Fall 2020

Chapter One

THE NEW (DISTRIBUTED) REALITY

When I sit down (or log into Google Meet) with a group of new JumpCrew hires, I always ask the salespeople the same thing. I ask them if they think we want them to be the best salespeople they can be. They all nod, and then I tell them they're all wrong. Then I explain why: no one aspires to work with, build a trusting relationship with, or buy from the best salesperson. We want our crew to be the best people, leaders, and businesspeople they can be. That's who I want to learn from, work with, buy from, and trust. Then I close the meeting by sharing insights from a wonderful *New York Times* article called "What Drives Success?"[1]

While so much of what we are trying to learn can seem complicated and overwhelming, what drives success can be broken down into a few elements that are clear and simple. So I share the results of a great study cited in the article, which found that three elements go into being great:

1. Great confidence in your skills and abilities.
2. Equally great insecurity in those same skills and abilities.
3. The ability to delay gratification, otherwise known as patience.

That's my way of letting new people know they're not just joining any old company. I let them know that my hope is they'll stay with JumpCrew for a long time and that we hired them because we believe in their ability to achieve great things. Now, while I mean those words sincerely, in reality I know they won't all make it, and I tell them that as well. People's desire for achievement is often in conflict with where they are on their journey and their capacity to work in an organization that holds them accountable for being their best. I share with them that at twenty-seven, I would have failed at JumpCrew with a 100 percent probability. It wasn't until I hit twenty-eight that I found my focus, and things changed. It was my time.

At JumpCrew, we respect the simple truth that some people won't be ready to do things our way, while others will. Our job as leaders is to take the people who have found their sea legs and their sense of self and give them what they need to grow into the best people they can be and to benefit from that growth for as long as we can.

That was our modus operandi before COVID-19, but the move to WFH forced us to rethink everything about how we led. Think about the typical office where everybody works face-to-face. The same people are present from Monday through Friday, so it's easy to develop a casual familiarity. But what's truly important is that work is a distinct environment from the home office, with its own set of rules and expectations. You can think about it in the same way you might think about an athletic field or arena where team sports are played—say, a baseball field or basketball court.

When a sports team is in the locker room, it's the same group of men or women as when it steps onto the field or court. But when the baseball players run out to their positions on the diamond, or the basketball players jog out to center court, something shifts. They're no longer a loose group wearing the same uniforms; now, they're a team gathered together in a specific place for one specific goal: *win*. The expectations and intensity, and the psychological feelings of mission and focus, are completely different.

In that environment, there's a sense of internal competition, of holding each other to high standards, of always having each other's back and not wanting to disappoint. There's a band of brothers sense that develops when you're part of a group that's triumphed over hardship and trauma and whose members are willing to walk through fire for each other. In those places and in those times, we draw energy from each other in ways we don't fully understand.

The in-person workplace operates by the same dynamic. When you walk into the office, you're leaving the other part of your life behind temporarily and, like an athlete, stepping onto the field of play. You and your peers compete even as you collaborate toward a common goal. You, too, have each other's backs. It's effortless to flow from one space to the next and connect with people about one topic or another, keeping multiple discussions going organically and simultaneously.

Because you're always around coworkers who aren't part of your family or normal social circle, you're constantly exposed to new people, ideas, ethnic traditions, political views, and the like. When you close a sale or nail a presentation, it's high-fives all around. When something goes badly, you've got people to commiserate with. You're fighting the same battles together. At the end of the day, you can turn off the lights and go home, like baseball players walking off the field after the final out. There's a clear boundary between the most important parts of your life.

But with the move to WFH, everything is different, and not just for rank-and-file individual contributors. Remote work has thrown management and executive leadership a huge curveball. What's expected from them has not changed substantively, but the conditions in which they're expected to deliver on those expectations could not be more different than they were as recently as 2019.

The Coercive Organization Is Dead

When you're running a department or company where your workforce is clocking in from home, the effortless chemistry and camaraderie of a shared space are gone. Maintaining something as basic as the flow of communication between colleagues requires more deliberate effort and planning. Before, updates on what was happening with a project might have been as simple as someone sticking their face into an office doorway to offer a quick heads-up. That made sense when such intrusions were predictable, normal parts of a day structured into a series of meetings and work periods shepherded by managers.

Not now. For remote workers, the day is an unbroken string of their own experiences, thoughts, and video meetings lacking social connection. There's no boundary between work and home life anymore, so the two bleed into one another. Zoom meetings break down when a housecat jumps onto a table; presentations get rebooked because a six-year-old needs to go to the dentist. In this environment, communicating and staying connected, which used to be so easy and natural, now feels intrusive. Slack conversations, text messages, Microsoft Teams meetings—they've become disruptions that *interrupt* work instead of being *part* of work.

This is the new normal that leaders face when WFH is no longer a desirable novelty. Leaders' need for meaningful, deep connections with their teams has never been greater. You can't bridge the physical distance between you and a struggling subordinate with a heart to heart or a quick pep talk in an empty office. Meanwhile, the need for building trust, personal connection, and a sense of shared culture is just as essential to a strong company as it was before the virtual work boom—maybe even more essential when you take into account some people's anxiety and distractions. When you boil all this down, three things have changed for leaders:

1. The importance of trust, connection, and culture to the health of the organization.
2. The best practices for growing those qualities.
3. The mental energy needed to grow them.

For most of the history of American business, trust, connection, and culture weren't regarded as mission-critical. They were fortuitous byproducts of a paradigm I call the Coercive Organization. There were always a few outliers—touchy-feely companies like Patagonia that treated employees' private lives with outsized consideration and respect—but for the most part, the model of leading hinged on supervisors occupying the same physical space as the supervised and exerting influence over their subordinates.

Let's return to the sports analogy for a second. If we rob a traditional corporate leader of the ability to be physically *there* in an office, it's a little like a baseball manager or head basketball coach trying to execute game strategy via a Google Meet link from his condo. When the coach is pacing the sideline or sitting in the dugout, all eyes are on him. His presence is palpable, and he can easily take a pitcher aside to remind him to keep his elbow up when throwing his slider or bench a small forward who blows a defensive assignment. Take that same leader out of his players' line of sight, and the effect is enormous. Physical presence lets leaders communicate and adjust behavior with a look, expression, or tone of voice.

We're all familiar with this coercive model of leading, which Daniel Goleman, in his theory of emotional intelligence, describes as toxic. It's the heart of a culture where the physical presence of autocratic leaders creates a carrot-and-stick narrative and where everyone toes the line mostly out of fear of being disciplined or losing their jobs. As Ajay Ramamoorthy writes on Upshotly: "Coercive leadership is explicitly evident when it's being implemented within a team. The style is often ruthless, overwhelming, and domineering. As humans, we value our freedom and even coercion based on authority may leave us feeling unpleasant and disgruntled. The employees start seeing their leader as unreasonable and demanding."[2]

The specter of the domineering manager hovering over the team bullpen and implying the threat of punishment becomes ridiculous when everyone's working from home. In fact, many of the fallback tricks of old-school command-and-control leaders, like Tom Peter's "management by walking around," lose their mojo in a WFH world:

- **Putting subordinates on the defensive with surprise appearances or requests.** Everything has to be scheduled now, and if an employee wants to be "too busy" for a call, he or she just blocks the time on the calendar and clicks "decline."
- **Appearing authoritative by being in position to lead a meeting or training session.** There is no front of the room in Zoom.
- **Relying on peer pressure to compel people to perform.** It's difficult to apply peer pressure when tuning out one's peers is a matter of turning off a webcam and muting the microphone.
- **The leader as fixer, the one with all the answers who can solve everyone's problems.** One side effect of WFH is that employees are forced to become more self-reliant, and with their growing confidence, they may not welcome the VP of marketing dropping in to impose her solutions on their situation.
- **Withholding social rewards as a way of enforcing discipline.** When the workplace was the center of easy social connection for many of us, the idea of missing out on happy hour or a company party was enough to keep a lot of folks working hard. No one's going to burn the midnight oil or work weekends to attend MS Teams trivia night.

Put simply, when leaders lose the workplace physical presence that empowers them to be coercive, coercion doesn't work. Working at a physical distance from their people amplifies the need for leaders to find other ways to motivate their employees—to create trust, connection, and a tribal culture in which people passionately *wish* to excel for reasons that have nothing to do with authority or the threat of punishment.

Few organizations are optimized to grow leaders, grow profits, and build community in this environment. Many, if not most, will have to see their way clear to a major cultural transformation if they are to duplicate their prior success in the new environment.

From "You Will" to "I Would Like"

This seismic shift in how organizations function has left many managers and executives ill-equipped to lead. As Arianne Cohen writes for the BBC, that's in part because the traits that have traditionally done the heavy lifting for face-to-face (F2F) leaders—charisma, extroversion, intelligence—don't translate to a WFH milieu. She says, "Instead, workers who are organized, dependable, and productive take the reins of virtual teams," she writes. "Finally, *doers* lead the pack—at least remotely."[3]

Put it this way: in the virtual world of work, the leader most likely to be effective is the leader who helps other people perform their best and *be* their best. Coercion is out. Coaching and inspiration are in. Out of necessity, leadership is becoming less about telling someone, "You will do this" and more about encouraging them to tell themselves, "I would like to excel for myself, my colleagues, and the community."

To achieve that, the new WFH reality is forcing many leaders to break the barriers between the personal and professional, demonstrate empathy, and expose their own human vulnerabilities, sharing more of their personal lives than ever and removing the protective armor that was standard issue in the physical workplace. It no longer benefits anyone to have executives, even the ones occupying the C-suite, seen as infallible or larger than life. Instead, they are being asked to invest not only in building rapport with their peers but also in building collegiality, care, and mutual respect with their teams and in assisting their direct reports in developing their own leadership qualities.

The atmosphere at JumpCrew is highly charged and competitive, even with everyone working from home. Expectations remain high. We're a sales organization where everyone knows hitting their KPIs is a must, and there's little tolerance for those who can't do it. Despite this, we have still managed to grow a culture built on unguarded, authentic human connection and deep self-reflection. This did not happen by accident.

Before everything changed, we were building out a 70,000 square-foot office and planned an August 2020 move in. Our plan called for us to grow out of that office in a year. Again, best laid plans. Our new plan is still TBD. It's possible we'll only have managers in the office with all of our teams working from home around the country. We'll be like a hive of Peloton instructors with our workers all over the world hunched over their sales dashboards instead of their bikes. There will still be sweat, but it will probably be flop sweat.

Instead of those shiny new offices, most of our people get together now in thoughtful, reflective online forums using a wonderful peer sharing and learning platform called Circl.es, which I'll go into with greater detail later. They inhabit a circular virtual space, which we will call a Circle, with people from different parts of the company, people they might not know all too well—or at all. They meet to explore the key drivers to success at JumpCrew, which differ for individual contributors and managers:

101 Topics for Individual Contributors:

- Driving results
- Developing resilience
- Becoming more adaptable
- Having a customer focus
- Being action-oriented

201 Topics for Managers:

- Driving results
- Communicating effectively
- Making quality decisions
- Managing complexity
- Ensuring accountability

Other topics in Circles include personal vulnerability, collaboration, and the challenges of working from home. With each topic, people share stories from their own experiences, listening to each other share, and asking questions to help each other see their actions and patterns more clearly. That's how you build connections and community when you're not in the same office.

If that doesn't sound like a way to build a hard-driving sales organization, you've probably watched *Glengarry Glen Ross* too many times. I'd struggled with growth mode more than once in past start-ups. We tried to grow as fast as humanly possible, and without process to follow, we were terrible about communication. If I had to start again today as a distributed organization, I would bake in training, check-ins, mentoring, partnering, and anything else that helps sales reps and other staff feel comfortable in their roles—and comfortable with me and other leaders. It's never been clearer that people won't follow a leader if they don't know where they are going.

I always account for the importance of people finding fulfillment in their work, and I make sure that learning what fulfillment means for each individual is imperative for every JumpCrew leader. That would help us better understand how to motivate and extract the best performance out of each person.

We've gotten JumpCrew to that point today by making the Pillars central to the company culture before WFH was ever on our radar screen. But since remote work became a necessity, those principles have become far more important to our survival and our continued growth than we ever thought they would be.

What we've discovered, largely by accident, is that in the virtual environment, it's even more important to discard the old definition of what it means to lead. Our outdated, top-down model of leadership was unreflective and—let's face it—egocentric. Leaders in that model enjoy wielding power and being the center of attention because it feels good to be in charge. If you're leading that way today, this book will make you uncomfortable.

But with WFH, you cannot intimidate, threaten, or lead through charisma and implied authority. You're trying to take employees who are their own virtual bosses, exercise absolute control over their environment, and probably lack connection with their peers, and turn them into a high-performing team that blows past normal expectations. To do that, you must help them be their best. You must position them to *want* to achieve great things for the organization out of a sense of community, belonging, and shared values. You have to inspire people to *love* the organization . . . and each other.

Learning Your ABCs

In this kind of enlightened organization, your ability to reflect, learn, communicate, collaborate, and endear yourself to others in a trusting and productive way will define your ability to be recognized, lead, and succeed. Personal growth and learning are vital components of what Peter Senge calls "personal mastery" in his book, *The Fifth Discipline.* Research from MIT's Sloan Business

School[4] surveyed HR professionals about the practices that could best help employees transition successfully to remote work, and the results were predictable (at least to me):

- Forty-seven percent of HR pros chose "Communicate frequently and well," making it the most widely chosen practice.
- Twenty-nine percent chose "Provide emotional and social support," including check-ins and supporting employee mental well-being.
- Twenty-four percent chose "Maintain productivity and engagement," which focused strongly on frequent virtual meetings and other tactics to keep employees engaged and feeling connected.

Of course, companies helping remote employees overcome the technical challenges of WFH was a big part of success as well (45 percent of respondents tagged it as vital). Still, the emphasis is clearly on soft interpersonal skills and policies that help people feel appreciated, informed, respected, and cared for. Coincidentally, that's a terrific description of an organization where coaching, culture, and connection are primary. But in addition to acquiring new knowledge and skills and communicating more effectively, beyond embracing the need for humility and patience, a higher level of importance is being placed on execution.

At JumpCrew, the sales dashboard—which was always important for individual motivation, measuring effectiveness, and scoring bragging rights—became our lifeblood. So while WFH offers a novel set of benefits from flexibility to greater work-life balance, results must, out of necessity, boil down to "But did you hit your numbers?"

A well-designed WFH organization contains systems to measure execution and use it as the new carrot. Of course, that can't be done with fear, or people will end up demotivated. The desire to execute, to deliver, is most effective when linked to a person's competitive nature. Wise leaders tie it to the welfare of the community of peers, teammates, customers, and leaders. People should want to execute, not because they will be fired if they don't, but because they don't want to let down the other members of the tribe, whom they care about and respect.

Execution-centrism also changes how we look at leaders. The cult of the CEO is an endangered idea in the WFH world because leaders have less ability than ever to grow their personal brands and maintain their mystiques through swagger and speechifying. Who cares? Now, it's about taking a workforce that might be distributed across ten time zones and using communication, compassion, and coaching to link them together as a single unit driving to hit their KPIs. Disgraced former WeWork CEO Adam Neumann couldn't do that, nor could disgraced former Uber CEO Travis Kalanick. Why? Because leading was all about them and the bluster and empty promises of the cult.

Leadership has *never* been about you, but now it's about you even less. Today's high-achieving organizations reward leaders based not on who *seems* like a leader but generally on performance, similar to the way Major League Baseball has stopped lionizing players who hit .300 with no power and started rewarding guys who deliver power and on-base ability, using stats like OPS (on-base + slugging). It's leadership, *Moneyball* style.

What sort of stats? Key performance indicators (KPIs) in the sales funnel not limited to new contracts per period, average conversion time, or qualified lead conversions; average contract value; average profit margin; customer acquisition cost; client retention and churn rates; and lifetime value. Equally important outside of the sales channel:

- On-deadline project delivery
- Hitting quarterly goals
- Employee retention
- Peer or customer Net Promoter Scores
- Employee engagement scores
- Advancement of your ILP (Individual Learning Plan)

Engagement scores are a terrific way to gauge the level and effectiveness of communication, collaboration, peer respect and trust, and support within the organization. The more employees feel connected with one another, listened to, and fulfilled in their jobs, the higher their engagement scores. What kind of metrics could you introduce into your org that would enable you to measure not only performance but also how reflective and compassionate people are?

Sustaining high performance means:

- Maintaining the continuity of your A players, the stars of your company who have the potential to be inspiring leaders.
- Supporting your B players, the talented people with the potential to graduate to A status, the ones whose growth you invest in.
- Exiting your C players, the hires who don't fit into your culture and can't step up to meet expectations, as quickly as possible.

Identifying people who won't succeed in an environment that is rooted in achievement and accountability is compassionate to them and to the rest of your team. The hire who doesn't fit can move on to a better situation while your A and B performers don't have to carry the weight of someone who can't do the job. Remember, any organization that can sustain a strong, vibrant culture while working remotely sets the bar high, growing faster with higher levels of employee satisfaction than its competitors. That only happens when the right people are on board and in the right seats on the team bus.

Papa's Got a Brand-New Bag

Some organizations have already adjusted to this new reality and are dominating in the WFH world. You've heard about Twitter, whose CEO, Jack Dorsey, told his people they could continue working from home "forever." Facebook's Mark Zuckerberg expressed the same sentiment. But there are many other companies that have adapted to WFH exceptionally well. Canadian ecommerce platform Shopify and freelance platform Upwork are among many successful and growing companies that appear to be thriving in a WFH environment, some going so far as to commit to partially or fully remote workforces for the foreseeable future. Job site FlexJobs identified twenty-seven category-dominating orgs that have embraced remote work as a long-term strategy, including Adobe, Amazon, Capital One, Microsoft, and Salesforce.[5]

Reaching those levels of accomplishment in a WFH world requires more than sliding a few new leadership clubs into your golf bag. It demands a new bag, a fresh set of tools that some executives may not associate with corporate leadership. But when your goal is to grow an organization that can thrive when even your superstars are working from home, this is the relevant skillset:

Radical candor. I fear too much empathy. Not because I don't believe it's valuable to be able to put yourself in someone else's shoes (it is), but because empathy can prevent leaders from saying what needs to be said and holding their people's feet to the fire. Kim Scott's best-seller *Radical Candor* offers a crystal-clear primer on walking the line between being aggressive and confrontational and squishy-soft. For me, that means setting clear expectations, both for individual performance and the collective JumpCrew experience, and then speaking with equal clarity about how those expectations are being met. If someone's falling short, you're honest about it with no judgment. Candor is about trusting people to receive unambiguous facts like grownups, not rendering a verdict on someone's character or future. You're not dodging hard conversations either. That does no one any favors.

Giving up being the problem solver. It's time to let go of the need to be the person with all the answers. Two components of the great remote organization—coaching culture and peer learning—expressly *remove* the executive or manager from the primary position as the one who fixes things. Instead, you listen, ask questions, share experiences, encourage, and sit back and let people find their own solutions. You will rapidly develop a deep satisfaction in watching your team grow and receive the dividend of growing with them.

Winning buy-in. In the past, "Because we said so" was a good enough rationale for any corporate policy. Not today. You're leading in a time when every person is the CEO of their own working life. You can't encourage autonomy and self-reliance with one hand and simultaneously take it away with the other. Instead, getting your team to enroll in your program is more a matter of sharing insight, giving voice to others, and winning fans. Give your people input on strategy; solicit their opinion about new initiatives. Give them the chance to make ideas their own, and they'll surprise you.

Cultivate grit. You're not here to coddle people. Do that, and you're treating them like children. Your goal is to build grit, the resilience that helps people get back up and keep going after a setback. Grit is your glue. Grit means, "Get it done despite all the other bullshit in your way." It's tough. But you're tougher.

Embrace skip-level management. To lead, you need a matrix of relationships at all levels, especially between people who may not normally come into contact with one another. Skip-level management means bypassing parts of the hierarchy to communicate directly with the people who make things run, whether that means moving down the org chart to individual contributors or upstream to the C-suite. People work for *people*, not companies. Skip level communication makes people uncomfortable and is not always popular, but when you're trying to survive a crisis, sometimes the best thing you can do is disrupt the status quo.

Size Matters

Whether it's a pure remote workforce or some sort of hybrid plan, you will also need to account for the One Hundred Rule. If your team is small enough, you can still manage it with some level of command-and-control style because you can also deal with each employee on a one-to-one basis. Once you approach one hundred people (a side effect of being successful), your organization becomes like a city that's gotten too populous for a volunteer fire department. In a larger organization, it becomes difficult to build trust, pride, and a sense of ownership on a person-to-person basis without face-to-face presence and the structure and process to support it.

What's possible in a WFH organization with fifty employees might be nearly impossible with two hundred and fifty. That's when you fall back on culture and community, which is what I've been talking about in this chapter. Also, the investment of capital and thought leadership into successful WFH increases as your org grows. Learning and development (L&D), planning, process development, training—as headcount grows, costs grow as well.

This is why so many promising young companies die or lose their momentum. They fail to invest in the organization beyond the leadership team. When opportunities arrive for the company to grow, everyone is trying to make the thousand micro-adjustments needed to innovate and stay aligned while things pick up speed. That's like trying to build a boat while you're sailing it. If your organization lacks a sense of community, and if they don't feel like they have a personal stake in the outcome, no one will do what it takes to onboard new hires, satisfy the new customers, or innovate.

JumpCrew was able to make the WFH transition with three hundred people pretty smoothly because even before WFH became a necessity, we were already operating with a higher degree of organizational-awareness and intimacy. That became clear to me as I prepped my speech for our JumpCon sales 2019 summit. I shared that the organization Rob and I had cofounded had become an organization where we felt like we had thirty cofounders. That's how invested and motivated the top 10 percent of our people were. If you want to maintain that intimacy in WFH, start while things are small.

The Power of Unlearning

None of this new model of leading comes easily or naturally. It certainly didn't for me. I stumbled through the early stages of WFH because I was still learning the importance of over-communication and personal connection with new hires.

In February of 2020, quite by coincidence, JumpCrew created a task force to figure out what software we would need to build to enable remote work, but the exercise was theoretical. The plan was for the distant future. Then the world changed, and we didn't change with it—not right away. When we first went remote, we just did it. We had three virtual huddles a day and focused on survival and performance. Teams struggled. Everyone missed the chemistry and energy of the office, and we didn't know how to replicate it. In the end, we literally transferred our culture, things like TED Talk Tuesdays and Sell a Donut Wednesdays, and made them virtual.

Working from home was a theoretical exercise for millions of corporate leaders until it wasn't. Now it's how we live. Many organizations won't go back to the way things were before because their workforces simply won't tolerate it. For you to grow into your potential as a leader in a distributed world, you have to forget the lessons of the pre-WFH world—to *unlearn* what you know.

Intuitively, a new manager is focused on delivering metrics, but today real-time reporting provides that. Today's enlightened leaders provide support and lead by example. They train, coach, and mentor people; ensure the availability of resources, data, and technical infrastructure; and champion reflective, communicative practices that foster trust and collaboration. That's what lets people be honest and hold each other accountable while caring about one another and the enterprise. That's what ignites innovation, not fear and coercion.

Doing that demands intentionality that didn't exist in the pre-WFH world. No longer can you as the leader rely on random encounters or morning meetings to do the heavy lifting of relationship building; now, you have to make the effort to reach out and connect, to let people know where you came from, where you are going, and what the expectations are. You have to schedule calls and Zoom meetings, Circl.es sessions, and check-ins. You have to lead consciously and deliberatively. It's harder. But it's more effective and more rewarding.

It's not all bad news; some things haven't changed much in the move to WFH. You still need focus, discipline, energy, and consistency. You still need to know how to motivate, and you still have to do what you say you're going to do. But you'll find that people will crave vision and purpose even more than when they were all in the office because a lot of them feel alone and isolated and want to feel connected to something bigger than their condo. They want to know that your organization is stable and growing and that they will have opportunities in the future. They want reassurance that leadership still has a positive outlook because that's part of what inspires them.

It's your job to make sure they get what they need and to do it from tens or thousands of miles away. Yes, there are risks to leading in this environment. Emerging leaders may never get the attention they deserve because they're not seen leading the troops into battle. But that's okay. It's not about you anymore, remember?

Anyway, this is the new normal. An August 2020 survey by KPMG found that two-thirds of the CEOs of large corporations planned to downsize their office space and make permanent shifts in favor of a remote workforce, according to CNN[6]. WFH is here to stay. The more you know about how and why leadership works in this environment, the better.

Chapter Two

THE SCIENCE OF REMOTE WORK

While working on this book, I was reading *Tribal Leadership* by Dave Logan and John King. It's a terrific book about how intraoffice groups come together around shared ideas and values, and it's especially relevant to the work from home situation we're navigating. Without the physical, motivating presence of leaders as connective tissue for the organization, a sense of tribal bond is what holds teams, departments, and entire companies together at a distance. Or, as Dave and John write, "Without the leaders building the tribe, a culture of mediocrity will prevail."[1]

Tribes build relationships between clients and themselves. For JumpCrew, our tribe is made up of us, our clients, and their customers. The goal is for the organization to be filled with wall-to-wall leaders in behavior and attitude, if not in title, people who go first, bring out the best in others, and set the example.

According to *Tribal Leadership*, tribes occupy five stages, often within the same company, and can evolve from one stage to the next:

Stage One: Despairing Hostility. Only 1 or 2 percent of tribes fall into this ugly category. Here, life sucks. These are street gangs, disparaging and hostile, and they band together for protection when they find each other. Cultural change at Stage One is critical and often requires swift and decisive change in personnel.

Stage Two: Apathetic Victims. About one-fourth of tribes have this culture. They're judgmental, resigned, and cynical, the people who fold their arms and watch things go wrong because they can't be bothered to care. Leaders at Stage Two try to protect their people from the intrusion of management. There is no urgency, accountability, or innovation. Think the DMV or the drones on *The Office*.

Stage Three: Lone Warriors. These tribes make up about half of office groups. They're defined by strong, smart, educated individuals who think knowledge is power and hoard it to win. The prevailing attitude is "I'm great, but you guys suck." These stars will outwork and outthink everyone else, but it's all about them and their egos, not the team. These power players are addicted to winning and tend to be resentful that others on the team aren't as competent or hardworking as they are.

There's a huge consulting industry dedicated to getting teams to Stage Three because it's easy to measure success on an individual basis. But it's dehumanizing. No amount of team building can turn a group of "every man for himself" players into a team. Somebody has to pass the ball.

Stage Four: Tribal Pride. Now we're getting somewhere. About 22 percent of groups slot in here. Here, the group means everything; if you take the tribe away, each person's sense of identity suffers. Leading this group is effortless because the leader feels carried along by the energy and passion of the group. This tribe always has an adversary—UCLA has USC, Apple has Microsoft—that brings out its best. This is the first stage where a group sees itself as a tribe and can produce greatness and stability.

Stage Five: Innocent Wonderment. This is the "life is great" stage, and it's only about 2 percent of cultures. This group has extraordinary chemistry and infinite potential to make an impact. They compete with what's possible, not another tribe. This is the team that produced the iPhone or got Apollo 13 home. Leading this tribe requires vision and inspiration.

One school of thought says that people naturally find their way to the tribal stage they're best suited for. That's dangerously fatalistic, especially in the WFH world. The job of the leader is to empower and inspire people to reach beyond their comfort zones—to find ease with self-reflection, candor, and vulnerability. That's especially true in WFH, where the leader's effectiveness depends entirely on his or her authenticity and ability to be a coach and a facilitator of trust, camaraderie, and communication.

Some of the initial success of WFH in 2020 was about novelty. But inevitably, novelty wears off, drudgery sets in, and people become disengaged. As the novelty of WFH disappears and the extraordinary becomes ordinary, leaders are in the business of maintaining energy and engagement without a physical workspace that allows peers and managers the luxury of immediate support, accountability, spontaneous collaboration, and social networking. How?

More to the point, can an understanding of the psychology and sociology behind remote work help leaders build better WFH organizations? I think it can, so let's do a deep dive.

Executive Function

If the Three Pillars feel a bit uncomfortable, there's a reason for that. In the modern era, leadership of any organization has been modeled largely on military leadership, which is in turn built on the idea of absolute authority. You, the leader, instruct your people, and they follow your commands without question. That makes sense on the battlefield where every issue is life or death, but not in the office where people relish a sense of agency and autonomy, the ability to solve their own problems.

Too many leaders still fall back on the military model, or what I like to call *amygdala leadership*. You probably know that the amygdala is an almond-shaped area of the brain that processes fight-or-flight emotions like fear and rage. Authoritarian leadership is about inducing those emotions in order to motivate and maintain order, and while that's bad enough in a traditional setting, it's disastrous in the WFH office.

Leading and growing a remote team effectively depends on set of cognitive operations that reside in a different part of the brain, the frontal lobe, and that are collectively known as *executive function*:

- Self-awareness
- Inhibition and restraint
- Nonverbal working memory, the ability to picture ideas and concepts in your mind
- Verbal working memory, the "internal monologue"
- Emotional self-regulation, the ability to use words, images, and self-awareness to see and control your emotions in real time
- Self-motivation
- Planning and problem-solving

Look closely at that list again. Problem-solving is the only function not expressly linked to the Aware Accelerated Organization because we're encouraging leaders to be coaches, not problem solvers. The others—meta-cognition, emotional control, healthy self-talk—are exactly the kind of functions you'd expect from a leader who is self-aware, restrained, emotionally open, and communicative. Great WFH executives enjoy strong executive function. Rather than use fear, anger, or envy to get people to do what they want, they unplug the amygdala and appeal to the higher levels of human nature.

While that sounds appealing, letting go of that amygdala-driven, militaristic mental leadership paradigm isn't easy. That's the model of leading we learned about in school and in our early jobs. It's become a habit, a neural pattern based on the brain's reward circuitry. Over the years, we've been programmed to find pleasure in the idea of giving orders and having someone carry them out. It's an ego boost. The secret to breaking this habit lies in something called *unlearning.*

Unlearning refers to becoming conscious that we are operating based on an unconscious habitual pattern of trigger and response, then choosing to set that pattern aside in favor of trying something else. As Mark Bonchek writes in the *Harvard Business Review*, "In every aspect of business, we are operating with mental models that have grown outdated or obsolete, from strategy to marketing to organization to leadership . . . Unlearning is not about forgetting. It's about the ability to choose an alternative mental model or paradigm. When we learn, we add new skills or knowledge to what we already know. When we unlearn, we step outside the mental model in order to choose a different one."[2]

Of course, unlearning everything you know about leading is a tall order. We have to start somewhere. So let's begin by questioning some common assumptions about work-from-home and why so many of us—myself included—were so against it for so long.

Transition

I asked JumpCrew CEO Rob Henderson how the company managed the transition from F2F to WFH with little prep time. He told me that the first step was deciding we would take things virtual. "That was on Monday, March 11," he said. "We had a client onsite who had been on a plane. In talking to the leaders who sat in a tiny conference room with them, I realized that we'd just had five people from Chicago in the office today, and at that point there were about eight cases of COVID in Chicago. That was how easy it was going to get [to Nashville]."

But before we could inform our employees, we had to give a lot of thought to how we would communicate with them. We didn't want them to panic over COVID or their jobs, and we also couldn't just issue one statement because not all people are the same. "We spent a lot of time talking through how people were going to respond to what we said to them," Rob says. "At the time, it was the more 'the sky is falling,' more 'here's how to take your laptop home and log into Zoom.' Then there was the business continuity side of things. How would we deliver products for our customers? So we were very deliberate about the messages we crafted for our teams and their leadership to help them understand the urgency of the situation."

Next, we took inventory. "We needed to figure out what we had and what people needed," Rob continued. "We sent out a survey asking things like, 'Do you have Internet at your house?' It doesn't seem like a question that you would have to ask, but there were people who didn't have Internet at home. A lot of people use a second monitor, so how were we going to get them the second monitors? We had to figure that out."

We managed to get everyone deployed safely to their homes, and we closed our office. Now, we had to see how this would negatively impact our business. And the answer was . . . not that much. Some people were filled with anxiety about the disease; others worried about their jobs and ability to be successful working around their families, roommates, or with the sounds of silence; and still others thought the idea of working from home was a great way to demonstrate their commitment and abilities—especially after yours truly had bashed the idea for so long. So Rob and I and the rest of JumpCrew's leadership wondered what challenges would present themselves.

For about two days, the move was controversial. Then it just wasn't. It was back to business. The teams had clear KPIs (that really helped us), and it was physically just as easy to hit those KPIs from home as from the office. Whether you're in a cubicle or on your couch, you're still making sales or customer service calls. You can still log into the sales dashboard. So the conversation switched to supporting the psychological and emotional well-being of our people.

How would they handle the isolation, the distractions, and the lack of social interaction? Would they stay motivated when they didn't want to work but couldn't go out because of stay-at-home orders? We had no idea, but that didn't last.

Rob says,

> Pretty quickly, people divided themselves into two groups. The first loved WFH. *This is great for me. This is what I've always wanted. This is my ideal job. I get to be in my pajamas.* Then the pendulum swung to the other extreme: the people who hated it. *I'm a social animal. I hate this. I've got kids screaming behind me. I can't focus. I've gained fifteen pounds in the last two weeks.* A lot of our top performers hated it. That was a problem because if our bottom performers had hated it, it wouldn't impact the business very much. But 20 percent of your performers are often driving 80 percent of your results, and when half of them hate working from home, you have a big problem. That was what we needed to manage.

If you know sales reps, you know what Rob means. They're often seen as gregarious, social animals who thrive on the energy of the room and the congratulatory high-five. We have a manager like that at JumpCrew, a type-A personality and sometime professional entertainer who would socialize with everybody and was incredibly popular. But he was also so hard-driving that if his sales reps tried to get up and go to the bathroom on the last sales day of the month, he could actually stop them. That kind of bond he had with his team, based largely on his charisma and charm, doesn't play the same way with people you have only met over Zoom. To keep him and others like him productive, we all had to adapt.

Rob started mandatory daily tactical meetings that, if we were in the office, we'd call "stand-ups" so we could continue having objective-based conversations. I held more intimate, voluntary lunches so everyone who wanted to could talk about what they were thinking and feeling. We also started seeing much more engagement on our Slack channels. We advanced to holding three general check-ins with our people every day, which later we realized was overkill, but our instinct at that time was to create moments of engagement deliberately and thoughtfully because they couldn't happen organically anymore. If we reached out too much, that was better than not doing it enough.

Community Can Flourish Remotely

This may be the defining characteristic of WFH:

Actions that were frictionless, automatic afterthoughts now take deliberation and planning.

I'm not talking about culture building, coaching or the other aspects of the successful remote organization. Those have always required a great deal of intentionality. I'm talking about the support, fun, warmth, purpose, and social activity—the sense of tribe and team community—that bonds people and creates community. Some of that is gone in a distributed organization, and reinventing it demands endless creativity and thoughtfulness.

We also have to ease up on the hype that WFH will ever replicate working in person. We all have to accept that Zoom happy hour won't ever create the same connection and sense of fun as live happy hour. It's often just another workplace obligation. If WFH is ever going to be a meaningful part of the future of business, then the new platform for connection is a shared learning experience.

Peer learning cuts deep. It's intimate and warm and meaningful. It's a part of doing your own work to be a better person.

The fact is, working from home is very much a double-edged sword. For example, a 2015 study from Stanford University[3] of five hundred employees working remotely over two years found that their productivity went up 20 to 30 percent while overhead costs dropped. Research by Global Workplace Analytics[4] found that WFH saved companies an average of $11,000 a year while OWL Labs[5] determined that overall, working from home makes employees happier.

Reams of additional research show that a majority of employees like working from home and would like to continue doing it at least part of the time. However, at the same time, WFH isn't all wine and roses for individual contributors. No one likes doing something because they have no choice. More to the point, remote work via Zoom or Google Meet can be exhausting. One experiment[6] found that while the constant gaze of a superior enhanced concentration temporarily, over a long period, it led to a higher risk of burnout. Also, breaches of etiquette are more common in remote environments because the in-person interactions, which help enforce social norms, aren't present, says Cal Newport in *The New Yorker*:

> In person, for instance, the social cost of asking someone to take on a task is amplified; this friction gives colleagues reason to be thoughtful about the number of tasks they pass off to others. In a remote workplace, in which coworkers are reduced to abstract email addresses or Slack handles, it's easier to overload each other in an effort to declare victory over their own rapidly filling in-boxes.[7]

If we're going to build thriving, vital organizations in a WFH future, we must begin by attenuating our expectations. Working from home will never be like working face-to-face. For some people, it will be a dream come true; for others, it will be a chore. We'll need new tools, new thinking, and new ways of being a community to make it work.

But the biggest issue with WFH appears to rest overwhelmingly with us—with leaders. Suspicion about what remote workers are doing when not being supervised has pervaded what used to be known as *telecommuting* since the 1980s. Executive reluctance about remote workers rests on all kinds of false assumptions:

- Working from home is synonymous with goofing off and not working.
- Team building and mentoring are impossible at a distance.
- It's impossible to predict which employees will excel in WFH and which will flop.
- People need the office for their social well-being.

There is probably some truth to the last one. Human beings want to be connected; the rise of WeWork and similar businesses is proof of that. Some research has found that working at home for long periods of time can lead to greater stress as people move less and have less psychological stimulation in their day. Studies[8] have shown that nearly one-fifth of WFH employees report feeling lonely and isolated, which makes sense when you consider not only how much time we spend at work but how intense our interactions often are. Chronic isolation is a serious health risk factor; research has found it to be twice as dangerous as obesity.[9]

Burnout is also an issue, especially as the clear boundary between work and home life is erased. A 2019 study by Digital Ocean[10] found that 82 percent of U.S. remote tech workers experienced some burnout, with more than half saying that they were working longer hours than their in-office colleagues. Four in ten felt that they had to do more and work harder than counterparts who were coming into the office.

Leaders can address these issues and find ways to compensate for them, but only if we acknowledge them and put programs in place. The reality is that in the future, when WFH is an option and not an obligation, workers will naturally sort themselves. We will have a group who are wired to thrive working on their own and another group who need the social fabric and personal interaction of the office.

However, without spontaneous interactions, and without intentional programs designed to create a deeper dialogue between people, culture building is impossible. Everyone becomes a silo. JumpCrew's commitment to online forums and heavily trafficked Slack channels celebrating everything from #parenting and #winning to #amplifyblackvoices predates COVID-19. It has allowed our community to grow stronger regardless of where people are located. As I'll keep repeating, the watchword is *intentionality*. Leaders can't be lazy anymore about building a culture because the natural bonding that happens when people are thrown together into a space with a shared mission is gone. We have to work at it. But it can and does happen.

Why Leaders Resist WFH

All the evidence suggests that when approached thoughtfully, WFH increases productivity. People learn to work smarter and more effectively when they're able to work at home, and they enjoy their jobs more. The trouble with WFH seems to be the biases, most of them outdated or irrational, that bosses have toward it. Many managers and executives just don't like it.

The people at the NeuroLeadership Institute have identified some common cognitive biases that keep many bosses from embracing WFH. One is the *safety bias*, which compels managers to worry more about the potential negatives in WFH (people shirking work) instead of the much more likely benefits.

Another issue is *expedience bias*, which leads us to reject options that are unfamiliar but might be superior. Because WFH "feels weird," we don't follow through with it.[11]

Leaders are also biased by our mental model of work or "work program," the mental patterns running in our heads. For many, work equals having an office away from home. That's a hard program to change, especially when you consider that many founders and executives have accepted the belief that they have less to gain and more to lose than the average individual contributor in switching to WFH.

A remote JumpCrew sales rep hired outside of Nashville won't get to hit the sales gong or go to happy hour, but in return, he has no commute, can spend more time with his toddler, and gets to work by the pool. It's pretty easy to sell WFH to that guy. However, our team leaders lose the ability to directly supervise their teams. They have to invest in new training and IT and rely on and trust in others. Their internal program says, "WFH is risky, stay where you are."

Leaders who expect to prosper have to understand and accept their own biases against what evidence shows to be a fundamentally positive change. Yes, it's a heavy ask. Your organization has to invest time and money creating a WFH strategy and ensuring that everyone has what they need to be productive at home. You have to recalibrate your professional methods and personal goals.

If you're still unsure that WFH is as beneficial as I'm saying, let's back that up with some data. Tracy Maylett, EdD, is cofounder of DecisionWise, a Utah-based firm that specializes in assessing and improving employee engagement—that quality where people are invested in their work with heart and soul and feel a real sense of passion and ownership for what they're doing. DecisionWise does huge engagement surveys, and I spoke with Tracy to find out what those surveys said about engagement before and after COVID-19 turned the world upside down.

"One of the questions we ask is, 'The level of stress in my job is manageable.' Overall, the average favorable rating—those who give that question a four or a five—is about 65 percent out of forty million responses," says Tracy. "Well, COVID-19 hits and all of a sudden, that drops down to 55 percent, but within one month it was back up to 66 percent favorable, people saying their stress is manageable. The number stayed that way for three months before starting to go down again (in May).

"Here's another one: 'I am confident that this organization has a successful future,'" Tracy goes on. "We got an 80 percent favorable overall in November of 2019, and that dropped to 75 percent after COVID hit. In April 2020, that jumped to 85 percent, then 89 the following month, and then back to 86." Those changes are statistical noise, and they don't obscure the pattern: Engagement increased during the early days of WFH.

Tracy takes a stab at why. "First, leaders are being much more intentional in what they do," he says. "Second is authenticity. You're seeing the real leader versus the face of the leader. You're seeing people show up in sweatsuits. You're seeing people stand up wearing shorts. And we're still trying to research this one in more depth, but there appears to be some gratitude for just having a job right now. And we're also seeing some degree of autonomy and trust that wasn't there in the past."

In other words, WFH works. The only thing standing in the way of you taking the leap is, most likely, you.

Getting Out of Your Own Way

Recently, I learned about two very different approaches to managing work-life balance in a WFH reality. One was by giant German conglomerate Siemens, which has about 380,000 employees. Their philosophy on gauging individual success and effectiveness in WFH is based entirely on outcomes. They don't care how you get the results, just that you get them. In a statement about letting employees work two to three days a week from wherever they wanted, CEO Roland Busch dropped this gem: "The basis for this forward-looking working model is further development [of] our corporate culture. These changes will also be associated with a different leadership style that focuses on outcomes rather than on time spent at the office. We trust our employees and empower them to shape their work themselves to achieve the best possible results. With the new way of working, we're motivating our employees while improving the company's performance capabilities and sharpening Siemens' profile as a flexible and attractive employer."

The bombshell word there is "trust." This is one of the world's largest corporations, and it's investing complete faith in its far-flung workforce. Impressive. Writer Justin Bariso calls the policy "a master class in emotional intelligence."[12]

Contrast that with a terrible approach put forth by a tracking software company called Prodoscore. This firm uses artificial intelligence to assess WFH employees based on the amount of time they spend clicking links and opening software apps—effectively, rewarding people for busy work, not results. Worse, they turn that data into a "productivity score" that's not only sent to each employee every morning, but that is compared with every other employee's score in a sort of remote, easily gamed survival-of-the-fittest scheme.[13] It's a punitive, insulting system overflowing with negative energy.

As you make the inevitable future transition into some form of WFH, your success or failure will hinge on your leadership team's ability to adapt to the changing demands, the policies and systems you put in place, and the kind of culture you support. Navigating that transition without sacrificing profits, people, or peace of mind means getting out of your own way, and that comes down to your answers to four questions.

First, was the move to WFH intentional (at least in part), or was it a reaction to events out of your control? This matters because how you frame the move is critical. Change is always unnerving even under the best of circumstances, so your employees not only need to know what's happening and why, but also that you're on top of it. If the move to WFH is a strategic, planned choice, then be clear about why, what the consequences may be, and what options your employees will have.

If the move is a response to external events, as it was with COVID-19, then the last thing you want to do is convey panic. Instead, be clear and open, but let your people know that you are adapting and formulating plans in real time to address the situation. You can even take a page out of Siemens' book and invite your people to offer their ideas and help with the transition, investing them with greater trust and strengthening your bond.

Second, does your existing culture enable or obstruct WFH success? Is that culture built around openness, accountability, autonomy, and learning, or authoritarian problem-solving? If it's the second one, accept the need for some radical changes or you will be very sorry. We were fortunate at JumpCrew that we already had baked the foundational principles of our company before the world fell apart. Because our culture was already built on intention and committed to encouraging authenticity, transparency, mutual respect, and shared values, it was relatively easy to port it from a F2F world to a WFH one using technology.

Third, are your communication tools, technology stack, and best practices defined and in place? Not everything is about hearts and minds. Some things are about if Aziz in marketing has the right software to review mockups online, or if Lenicia in customer support has fast enough Wi-Fi. As soon as you know you're going remote, three of your first tasks should be:

1. Determining the essentials your people *must* have in order to carry out company business productively and professionally from home;
2. Doing a complete tech inventory of every employee to determine what they have and what they need; and
3. Communicating and demonstrating the new expectations for frequency and depth of communications.

Finally, do your employees have sufficient support in getting set up and dealing with the new environment? Are you checking in with them multiple times to make sure they have what they need in terms of IT, office furniture, and so on? Are you getting a read on how they're handling the isolation and lack of work-home guardrails? Are you expecting them to be up and running in a week, or are you giving some of them a long leash so they can adapt?

Workers in Wonderland

There's a fifth factor here, and it's you. How will *you* adapt to the change, voluntary or not? Leaders face many potential challenges in the move to WFH: fear, difficulty adapting their leadership style, problems holding people accountable, questionable communication skills, and a reluctance to fire people who can't make the leap. Everything runs downstream from leadership, so if WFH in any form is going to work, it has to begin with the people in the C-suite, senior executives, and departmental managers.

Time to start thinking like a picky diner in a restaurant and develop a taste for more effective substitutes to the more common top-down management approaches:

For top-down authority, substitute "regulated autonomy." At JumpCrew, tools like sales dashboards gamify quantitative aspects of performance—i.e., numbers of calls and talk time—and allow teams to self-manage their pace relative to their peers. Leaders have to hone their emotional intelligence to implement the right balance of check-ins and oversight to allow people to self-direct but still hold them accountable. Great organizations typically don't need leadership to manage activities because our teams are smart enough and motivated to look at them on their own. We need leadership to think about improving the behavioral outcomes of the actions and provide the feedback that improves products and process.

For hierarchy, substitute "democracy." The hierarchy still exists in a WFH, but it's much less apparent. Virtual all-hands and casual meetings where people are live chatting alongside the speaker empower engagement, help everyone feel part of the decision-making process, and break down barriers of communication between individual contributors and management. Leveling the communication playing field encourages collaboration, demonstrates leadership at every level of the org, and promotes the emergence of new leaders. For example, one of our warm-up exercises for Circles is to ask everyone to share their "weather report," only this weather is internal. How are they feeling? What's their energy? What's their mood? That might not appear to matter in a F2F office, but it's crucial in WFH when it's easy to feel like you're working in a silo.

For Tom Peters's "management by walking around," substitute "psychological safety." To some individual contributors, managers walking around is the anxiety-inducing equivalent of management-by-ambush. Now, all communication is either scheduled or transparent, so it's easy for employees working at home to control the engagement and not be surprised and off-balance. Using tech, they can also maintain communication "back channels" that let them chat with colleagues during meetings, and that's something you should both encourage and ensure are safe from eavesdropping. Either you trust your people or you don't. In the end, there is a fine line between motivating outreach and intrusive coercion. Each organization and leader has to identify where that line is for themselves.

For a rigid schedule, substitute "flexibility and patience." Most leaders *hate* this one because they loathe the notion that kids, dogs, and Amazon deliveries require urgent attention at times during the workday. But they do. In this new world, time is fluid while both deliverables and sometimes deliveries are not. The old markers that cued us to the passing of the workday—the morning meeting, lunch, afternoon coffee, 5:00 p.m.—are history. Now, work is about managing distractions. Also, it's equally important for the organization to respect people's privacy and home lives as much as you expect them to respect the company's needs. Spontaneous calls and meetings can be easily precipitated with an unobtrusive Slack or text: "Can you talk now?"

For every man for himself, substitute "help with the home office." Cox Communications, an Atlanta-based telecom with about twenty thousand employees, invested millions of dollars to help every worker get what they needed to trick out their home workspace. That's a smart move. Downtime, especially in sales, is murder; your WFH transition must minimize it. As part of the recruitment process, teams should confirm that the candidate has a quiet and professionally acceptable space with sufficient bandwidth. Equally important is the org's responsibility to make sure every one of your people has the computer, monitors, keyboard and office equipment they need—even a comfortable chair. That's a small price to pay for continuity of business.

Above all, connection remains a high priority. Water cooler talk as we remember it is gone. It's harder in WFH for your people to walk over and tap you on the shoulder when they need help and advice, so the risk is that they don't ask. Therefore, it's more important than ever for leaders to create thoughtful opportunities to build meaningful connections with their teams outside of work meetings—and *especially* outside of virtual "happy hours." Those became a thing during quarantine, but they add little or no value unless they're thoughtfully constructed. It's a better use of your time to put together a small team and think through activities that let small online groups open up, share their hobbies and interests, and take their work relationships deeper than they could in virtual meetings.

Accountability Is Everything

In the interest of staying connected and creating new connections, I got out of my comfort zone in 2020 and started showing up for Zoom meetings five minutes before the scheduled start time so anyone on the calls could hang out, talk about their day, tease each other about their haircuts, and bond. I never would have been comfortable with that before COVID-19. But the virtual meetings tend to start on time without social dialogue, and this practice put that personal connection and openness *into* my comfort zone.

It's a new world. Leaders must become comfortable with getting more personal. Emotional intelligence, or EQ, can be as important in leading a WFH org as an MBA. As someone who doesn't have an MBA, I'd argue that EQ has more leadership value. You'll need to learn to "read the room" and assess what helps people relax and engage in a virtual format. I've heard stories of CEOs taking virtual meetings while on exercise bikes and a JumpCrew manager doing important calls on their phone while in the grocery store checkout line. Those examples of disengagement aren't likely to end well. It's not just your employees who have to commit to this. You do too.

There's a flip side to this, however. *Accountability.* Accountability is what makes WFH work. It's is the price of flexibility, of the freedom to work in your sweats and take breaks to walk your dog to your favorite taco place. If people working remotely don't hit their KPIs and meet their goals, the entire enterprise falls apart. Trust withers, and without that, WFH isn't possible. No one will give their best effort remotely when they fear that no one else is being held to the same high-performance standard.

Everyone must become comfortable with the expectation of delivering measurable outcomes. It's your job to come up with ways of measuring performance in your corner of WFH heaven. If you're inherently a sales org like JumpCrew, that's easy because your people have sales KPIs. In other parts of the organization, you could be looking at projects finished, deadlines met, client responses, money saved, patient outcomes, NPS scores, or any of a hundred other metrics.

Figure out what works for your business and implement it. Accountability goes hand in hand with communication, vulnerability, authenticity, and ultimately trust because when people feel that the company cares about them, they're far more likely to care back—to agree to be held to stringent performance benchmarks. They won't feel that accountability is punishment; they'll feel like equal partners in making sure the trains run on time.

Creating culture is like cooking. Add the ingredients and apply your skill, but your methods will differ depending on the outcome you are trying to achieve. Some organizations need a light sauté, while others need to be buried in a pit with hickory logs for twenty-four hours, Kansas City barbecue style. The outcome will be a blend of your ability, your recipe, the quality of your ingredients (your people), and luck.

The demands of WFH have shown us that not all organizations are built to run hard. Lots of people (maybe most) don't want to be held accountable and pushed. Building an organization that does want those things means hiring the right people and building an accountability culture where peers and colleagues insist on the best from each other, and everybody complies because they love the work and the tribe. That takes time. You can't just drop these ideas on people in a materially different culture and expect them to get it and enroll in the new program.

Start slow. Celebrate small wins and give yourself a break. Remember, it's no longer your job to be the fount of all knowledge or the disciplinarian. Now, your job is to create an accountability structure and be a center of calm, rational decision-making. To provide clear direction and expectations. To facilitate continuous, healthy communication. To create a space of psychological safety where everybody can be themselves and feel seen, listened to, and esteemed.

Leadership in WFH isn't setting a goal and checking progress; we have software and dashboards for that. Optimal long-term results no longer come from direct application of force. Success in WFH calls for *jujitsu leadership*. You get results by inspiring people who *want* to achieve, helping them tap into their intrinsic motivation, empowering growth and self-determination, and holding them to account. Bring that to a group of people who share a common vision, and you'll create a powerful collaborative community. Your organization's ability to do this will define its ability to innovate, transform, and succeed.

Chapter Three

PILLAR NUMBER ONE: REFLECTIVE LEADERSHIP

Who looks outside dreams; who looks inside awakes.
—Carl Jung

Some time ago, I attended my annual entrepreneur forum retreat. One fellow entrepreneur who had successfully sold his business, someone you would expect to be filled with relief and excitement, was struggling with what would come next. He was stuck in the transition zone between where he was when he left his last business and where he had wanted to go for years. More importantly, he had written his personal playbook in reverse order. Instead of leveraging the confidence from his success to fuel his next business, he was overwhelmed by a lengthy list of self-doubts.

As he became more successful, his list of reasons why he wasn't grew longer. My challenge was to help him delete the list. But there were other equally successful entrepreneurs in the same forum, and it seemed like he was looking to his peers' progress to validate his own *lack* of progress. Lack—of success, of status, of self-worth—seemed to be a pattern or cycle that had become part of his program or identity. It was a program that might have once motivated him but had long since stopped and was now holding him back.

Entrepreneurs tend to be driven, positive people with a confidence bordering on arrogance. But being a successful entrepreneur is about tapping into that positive, emotional core that you have and building on it with each venture. Success begets success. What's more, your ability to do that in a collaborative environment is even more powerful because individual contributors feed off your energy as you feed off of theirs.

Today, leaders who cannot share their thoughts and their feelings are more vulnerable than ever. For decades, business has revolved around the unique set of rules that seem to apply only to executive leadership—call them "executive privilege." Occupying an office in the C-suite gave you a get out of jail free card that excused all manner of personal shortcomings, from a lack of empathy to wretched communication skills. Even when you gutted team morale with a flash of temper or made a terrible strategic call, you could fall back on your implied authority so long as you hit your numbers.

WFH has pancaked the idea of leading with old-fashioned authority like asphalt under a steam roller. Adolfo Velasquez, a senior vice president at JumpCrew, told me, "When we closed the office, a new set of people got seats at the table. When leadership is not predefined by proximity and walking around, the best communicators get the seats because they are the most proactive. Really engaged folks are figuring out a way to over-communicate regardless of the distance. They are the ones who don't lose their voice and seats and gain standing. The nonverbal leader, larger than life, in-person communicators don't really matter anymore."

Precisely. Success in this environment comes down to one commandment: Know thyself. A tiny fraction of leaders naturally possess the self-awareness to understand and accept their weaknesses, the ability to see themselves as others do, and the meta-cognition to manage their thoughts, feelings, and responses in real time. The rest of us grope around in the dark and try to learn something as we go. Reflective qualities are *acquired wisdom*. You'll acquire them not through classes and seminars, books, or even experience but through deep, sometimes painful, reflection on your experiences, self-discovery, and acceptance of your own weakness and fallibility.

The heroic leadership journey is about looking at yourself. That's what Brad Reedy writes about in his book *The Journey of the Heroic Parent*. It's the same journey that enables inspirational leadership. The only place we can go to make certain changes is inside—and you may not love what you find. That's our most important work. There are many different roads to truly seeing yourself. Some of us are successful in self-reflection using mindful meditation, some have great coaches, and still others like me are lucky enough to connect with great therapists. Our ability to see others is a critical part of leading, but it is based on our ability to see ourselves.

I have not always embodied those qualities. Neither have many of the leaders I've known. Often, they've had no incentive to change. The system rewarded their behavior—good or bad. Now they have incentive. *We all do.* Reflective leadership is not something you're born with. But it can be learned. So let's learn.

The Smartest Guy in the Room?

Once upon a time, I worked in Hollywood. I started my career partnering with Doug Liman, who's become a top Hollywood director responsible for hits like *Swingers* and *The Bourne Identity.* I produced his master's thesis film at USC, and after that, we made a feature film that you've never heard of, and I fell victim to what I know now was an enormous lack of self-awareness—more plainly, a total disconnection from reality.

We worked on our feature film for two years and made no money. I had to sue people to get my salary. I didn't know what I didn't know, and I arrogantly put myself in a situation that I wasn't prepared for where my role was marginalized and I was in over my head. It got deeply ugly, but beyond that, the details are irrelevant to our discussion. Suffice to say, I passed on working on Doug's next project, which became *Swingers,* but that was the right call for me. Doug and I have long since repaired our relationship and are close friends now, and the experience proved invaluable. But at the time, it was my most humiliating failure. Even so, I walked away thinking my future was made, when in reality, I had no next career step. What I did have was a wake-up call.

Unemployed for months, I experienced my first bout of depression, which led me to think much more carefully about what I was doing and why. So much of what we go through when we're younger, even though it can be hard and humiliating, is invaluable because it teaches us to pause, swallow our pride, ask questions, and learn. I also benefited from the work of a good therapist, who helped me push through the hardest parts.

I realized that I had skipped too many steps. I had jumped from working as a production assistant—a PA, the lowest person on any set—to producing a feature film. Without the experience or wisdom to fake it well, I flopped and ended up working as an assistant to a high-profile producer who thought communicating meant screaming nonstop. In 1995, with my twenties careening to a close and with no vision for a successful career in film, I searched for a different kind of opportunity. One where my own hard work would directly result in a payoff. I took an entry-level sales job at a temporary staffing company.

It was my first opportunity to prove that I had the grit to do a hard job and do it long enough to make something good happen. Meanwhile, my friends who had real plans and focus were already making things happen. Instead, I sat my ass in a chair making cold calls for nearly two years until I found a method of success—a way to understand and channel my aspirations and my dreams in order to take the right steps forward. If I had written a book before Jump-Crew, that would have been the book.

I reached my inflection point at twenty-eight years old. What changed? *I changed.* I had been a short-term thinker and was quick on my feet, so I naturally thought I was smarter than everybody else. Then I learned (the hard way) that there are no shortcuts. You've got to put your ass in the chair and do the work. Most important, you have to know why the work matters and if the work is taking you someplace you actually want to go. If you don't, you might look up in twenty years and say, "How the hell did I get here?"

If you think you don't need this because you have a high IQ or an Ivy League degree, you're wrong. You might need it *more* than the average Joe like me. Being the smartest guy in the room doesn't matter. Intelligence and education can get in the way of honest self-inquiry because self-inquiry is unnerving, even frightening. Like the CEOs who rely on traditional power or the ability to instill fear and see success, you are less likely to be reflective about achievement when it comes as a result of natural gifts. Being "a natural leader" becomes your program.

The trouble is, the more implied success you have, the more the program reinforces itself, leading you to a place where you perceive the risk of change or discomfort as being greater than the risk of ignorance. The irony is, by settling for success based on ability without developing your self-knowledge, you'll never know how much more successful you could have been. Leaders like this suffer from the curse of some success, the belief that things will always trend better for them. That works—until the trend line plummets. Then those leaders are exposed and can end up stuck without people they can count on, maybe broke or disgraced by their own arrogance.

Intellect doesn't matter. Cleverness doesn't matter. Education doesn't matter. Network doesn't matter. None of it matters until you possess the ability to look at yourself, honestly and without judgment, and see where you are sabotaging yourself and others. In self-inquiry, the intent is not to fix or solve but to understand.

Changing Your Operating System

Moving from *reflexive* to *reflective* allows us to find peace, confidence, and self-compassion, creating alignment in our relationships. We identify and ultimately eliminate the parts of our personal programs that are no longer helping us. That's meaningful change. Being reflective means to see yourself as others do—to pause, to think, to question your motivation before you decide, and to look back before you go forward. It doesn't mean being passive or indecisive. When you stop looking for evidence that supports your argument, you start to see the whole picture. That's when change happens. You see the code in your program that isn't working.

What are programs? They're behavioral patterns that repeat and become a part of who we are—our identities. Over time, it becomes difficult to parse what programs are still beneficial and which have outlived their utility. In the case of leaders, the reward for letting the program take charge might be pride, power, prestige, material comforts, or all of the above. When those rewards become enticing enough, we become programmed to protect—not change, innovate, or evolve—our behavior. When those patterns cease to serve us and start to yield negative outcomes, they can be called addictions.

The WFH world has revealed the deficiencies in our programs in radical, unprecedented ways. Constrained, reactive behavior is ironically harder to hide when everyone is working at home. Interactions are not just wildly different now, but they can play out in endless new combinations like the ones in a choose-your-own-adventure book. Many of the old programs are obviously no longer working. Knowing yourself and leaning into the change that enhances your programs, your words, behavior, and presence is new leadership currency. The infallible leader is out. Leading with an apology, acknowledging what you don't know and asking for help—these are the currency of leadership in the new normal.

If you are struggling with clarity around decisions people you trust are seeing clearly, or sometimes feel rudderless trying to lead in a new role or WFH organization, your old programs are probably controlling your thoughts, words, and actions more than you'd care to admit. Two programs are running within all of us, simultaneously, all our lives. The *program of origin* is Darwinian, woven into our DNA. Its applications enhance things like survival and procreation: fight or flight, aggression, the impulse to follow strong leaders, the urge to fear what (or who) we don't know. Not exactly the best traits to advance achievement and collaboration in the modern workplace.

The other program is *family of origin*. This is the psychological and emotional baggage we've carried since childhood, piled on us by our parents, friends, school, and past work experiences. If, like me, you grew up in a house full of opinionated people who already knew what you would be good or bad at and had been sharing it with you since you could talk, you might spend a lot of time searching for the adult version of that person before you stopped and said, "Well, hell, maybe they didn't know what they were talking about!"

Childhood, when the brain is incredibly plastic, is when our family program hardens. Never scoff at the idea of the "inner child." That child is the reason we either accept or suppress our emotions and why we fear some things while confronting others. Conflict, hardship, abandonment, even raised voices—these cause trauma that many of us never resolve. It's easier and safer to bury it, but it can haunt our relationships, and deep into our professional careers, it can impact our ability to achieve.

Those early experiences lead to unconscious beliefs about ourselves, the world, and our place in the world, some of which are limiting, disempowering, even crippling subconscious stories:

- "I'll never be good enough."
- "I don't deserve success."

- "Nobody will ever believe in me."
- "I don't have what it takes to get the job done."

We don't often realize it, but our words, choices, actions, and outcomes often stem from those beliefs. That's why this is "programming." Our default behaviors and beliefs are like the operating system of a computer, unseen but controlling. That's why everything starts with becoming reflective. Only when you hear your words, see your actions, and feel your reactive responses will you question if they're valid and useful. Only then will you do the hard work of challenging and changing them. Only then will you become the leader you can truly be.

Holding a Wolf by the Ears

I spent my childhood in a loving, overbearing Jewish household, and while guilt was a primary motivational tool, it was also instilled in me that I could be whatever I wanted (except president, but who would want that job these days?) through the virtue of hard work. However, my parents also convinced me that our family wasn't good at language or math, so I wouldn't be either. My father also liked to joke that his father had called him a "lazy good-for-nothing" and then call me the same. With that program running in the background of my brain, I limped along in school, convinced that being bad at math and being a slacker were beyond my control, woven as they were into my DNA double helix.

What rubbish. Years later, I would more than dispel all the assumptions—especially that I was lazy—as I reassessed much of my family program and started to benefit from the confidence that comes with choosing change and recognizing your own potential.

I also committed to doing my own inner work, unpacking the bags that led to thoughtless and emotional reactions and limited what I could achieve.

Doing the work. There's a loaded phrase. It suggests a subculture of therapy, meditation, or even wilderness retreats designed to understand emotions and act on them, not bury them. It's easy to snicker at such programs as touchy-feely . . . except that *is* the work.

- Digging into past traumas.
- Accepting who we are.
- Questioning what we believe about ourselves.
- Learning to embrace our emotions instead of fearing them.
- Being vulnerable and fallible and real and seeing those qualities as signs of power, not surrender.

That's the work, and if I talk about it from a male frame of reference, that's only because I'm male. Regardless of gender, that is the true work of any leader who aspires to lead a great remote organization. All leaders have a responsibility to do their own work. Seeing programs for what they are and freeing ourselves from their auto responses accelerates our ability to lead and achieve. It improves our relationships, creates trust, and allows people to trust in us and collaborate with us. Our ability to see and lead others is based on our ability to see and lead ourselves.

However, it's hard to view yourself objectively. Don't feel bad; the problem is universal. As part of a published study assessing the health risks of three hundred married couples, researchers also asked the couples to rate themselves and each other on hostile personality traits like anger and antagonism. Overwhelmingly, the study found that in self-reporting, people underestimated their hostility, but their spouses assessed those qualities accurately.[1] Many other studies with such groups as military officers and subordinates show the same effect: our egos and belief systems don't want us to pull back the curtain. If your sense of identity is built on denying the ugly, painful parts of your psyche, you'll prevent your conscious mind from confronting them at all costs. As the old saying goes, the truth hurts.

The result is like the proverb about holding a wolf by the ears: *You don't like it, but you don't dare let go.* When we live unaware of the programs that drive our behavior, we're literally living unconsciously. The fear or emotional pain we don't address, understand, and accept inevitably transfers to the way we lead others. And when you lead without self-reflection, when your emotional triggers drive your reactions, you'll only get results while you're in the room. That brand of leadership doesn't breed trust, loyalty, or community, so as soon as your back is turned, your people will always, always, *always* do less than their best. Because you haven't given them a reason to care.

Remember, people don't work for organizations. They work for people. If you want your people to care about the organization, they have to care about you and *the team.* When the leaders on your team all share this outlook, and when the other teams in the organization share it as well, then the organization becomes a community.

The Servant Leader

Hamdi Ulukaya is a Turkish immigrant who came to the U.S. in 1994. You might never have heard of him, but you know his product: Chobani, the bestselling yogurt brand in the country. Back in 2005, Ulukaya bought a shuttered yogurt factory from Kraft Foods and began making his own yogurt based on the traditional recipes from Turkey and Greece. Obviously, the strategy was a success; 2018 revenues were about $1.5 billion and continue to rise.

But Ulukaya sees himself as more than a CEO. Like many reflective leaders, he knows that his platform and visibility give him the opportunity to affect real change. His cause: immigrants and refugees. He's made hiring refugees and immigrants his personal mission, saying, "The minute a refugee has a job, that's the minute they stop being a refugee."[2] He also encourages other chief executives to do the same, insisting that the work ethic and fierce motivation of immigrants and refugees will help drive companies' success.

Unsurprisingly, this advocacy drew the wrath of anti-immigrant forces starting in about 2016. Ulukaya received threats, as did his facilities. But he hasn't backed down, and in 2016, he rewarded his employees for standing by him by giving them 10 percent of the company. Giving and serving those who make success possible is simply part of his business philosophy: "Large companies like ours have a greater responsibility to the people who've contributed to our success . . . for the sake of our communities and our people, we need to give other companies the ability to create a better life for more people."[3]

That's *servant leadership*, and it's at the heart of being a reflective leader. When you find the courage to look back and look within, you start to see your flaws and weaknesses. Are you smarter than most of the people in your company? Maybe. Better educated? Perhaps. More experienced in operating and growing a dynamic organization? Probably. But upon reflection, you can see that the areas where you're superior aren't inborn talents; they're stuff you learned through hard experience, through risk and failure. That means, given the same opportunities and connections, lots of your coworkers could be just as or more successful as you are in their own unique ways. That's humbling, and it should be.

Humility leads to empathy, letting you see other people from their own perspective—challenges, worries, hopes, fears, you name it. With your defenses down and your heart open, the needs of other people and your ability to make a positive difference in their lives becomes your mission. Sure, your primary responsibility is to grow a resilient, profitable business, but like Hamdi Ulukaya, you start to see that the two goals are the *same* goal.

How do you practice servant leadership? It's a state of mind more than a practice. Leadership stops being a system for satisfying your ego and bolstering your self-esteem. It becomes a means for reaching your full potential as a human being by helping others reach theirs. Like a great martial arts sensei or philosophy guru—or a great parent—servant leaders find satisfaction and self-expression when their students blow past them to become even more accomplished and happier than their teachers. You don't stop caring about your own advancement and reward; you just stop seeing your own success and the success of the people you lead as separate things.

They're not. They're the same.

Deep Dive

Ideas about reflection and self-awareness have a strong link to the Buddhist tradition. One of the fundamental tenets of Buddhism is reflection on who we are and on our "basic goodness"—the idea that we are inherently complete and worthy. That's a refreshing contrast to a society that tells us we can only be worthy—of love, belonging, or whatever—if we change ourselves or meet someone else's expectations.

The philosopher John Dewey also plays a role in defining reflection. To him, it was a form of problem-solving, a deliberate cognitive process triggered by someone's hesitation or doubt. Reflection for Dewey involves observation, developing possible solutions to a situation, and testing them for effectiveness. Call it "scientific mindfulness" if you like.

Turkish educators Süleyman Davut Göker and Kıvanç Bozkuş nicely summed up the philosopher's take on reflective leadership when they wrote, "Reflection is a vital component of leaders' daily life, not a detached or disconnected action but primal, promoted by the culture and structures of an organization, which affects choices, policies, and decisions together with the emotions and politics related to them. Considered from this angle, to be reflective should not be considered as a method, which has been acquired and occasionally used, but an inherent component of what to manage or lead means."[4]

Doing the Work and Other Things that Make a Reflective Leader

One of the many things that impressed me about JumpCrew CEO Rob Henderson was how he responded to the transition to WFH by becoming more reflective, mindful, and compassionate toward our employees and himself. Rob's younger than me, and reflective leadership is often an older person's game. It takes years to sift through the detritus of failure and blame to come to the conclusion that "Maybe I need to stop running from my needs and my demons and start leaning into them." It took me decades to get there. Rob got there faster. That's impressive.

During summer 2020, I had a conversation with Rob. "Six months ago, I wouldn't have called any employee out of the blue, period," he told me. "It was only about business. After everything happened, I realized that I needed to call people just to say, 'Hey, I'm calling to see how you're doing.'

"Also, when COVID started, I was telling everybody, 'You have to be on video because it's important for people to see you,'" he continued. "I think there is some truth to that in, in the right circumstances. But in other circumstances, you are just burning yourself out by sitting there, in your chair, staring at the computer screen all day long. You're more likely to have a normal conversation if you're walking around your backyard, your driveway, or whatever it is that you have do. I have definitely found that to be true for myself."

That's getting far enough outside yourself to observe yourself living out the patterns and dynamics that don't serve you. It's hard work in the most placid of times, and Rob hasn't been leading an org in placid times. That example points to the essential definition of a reflective leader:

· ·

Someone willing to do the work.

· ·

Putting in the work is huge because simply by admitting that something is impairing your ability to be happy and lead others, that you're flawed and willing to go to uncomfortable places and be vulnerable, you're already halfway to being reflective.

"Doing the work" means looking at your past with clear eyes and honestly confronting any experiences or traumas that shape your identity and interactions to this day. It means examining whether your behavior at work is serving your goals. Is your goal to lead a team and inspire greatness, or is it to self-aggrandize and feel import-ant, or perhaps to prove to someone—or yourself—that you're worthy of respect and esteem? Any agenda that's not about making everyone better and creating trust and community is counterproductive.

Doing the work means seeing any patterns you've been obeying mindlessly and how they shape your words, actions, and outcomes. It means recognizing that your thoughts and feelings are not facts; they are just thoughts and feelings. It means confronting the reality that your deepest beliefs may be self-delusions intended to shield you from the consequences of your questionable choices—people you screwed over, ethical lines you crossed, time you didn't give to your family, or failures you can't own.

Doing the work means coming face to face with all of it . . . and then letting yourself off the hook by remembering that you're doing the best you can with what you have, and that you're here, now, trying to do better. That's all you can do, and that's enough. But remember that until you do it, you're going to keep wounding other people unintentionally. As the brilliant coach Jerry Colonna says, "The cost of your unpacked bags is paid by those with whom you spend your days." Unpack those bags.

After my wife died, my work involved exploring and letting go of the idea that I was complicit or responsible—that I had control over her cancer and had failed to protect her, and I was therefore not worthy of feeling good about myself. As my therapist would ask me every week, "What crime did you commit?" I struggled with this until I realized that how I thought about myself was connected to how I was behaving toward other people and the impact that behavior had on them.

One day, I told Rob Henderson, the then VP of sales for Local-Vox, that he should be more generous with compliments to his team. He responded by saying, "Why? Not giving compliments seems to be working for you." Ouch. But he was right. This was an era of my life when I had a lot of rage over what I had lost and the mistakes I had made. It was only through years of therapy, which I clutched like a life preserver after my wife's death, that I was able to weather the crisis and accumulate enough self-awareness to write this book.

Rob's biting, brutally honest feedback was almost as valuable as that therapy. It helped me recognize and celebrate my own successes and practice demonstrating more appreciation for others. But what else makes a reflective leader? The reflective leader demonstrates mastery of:

Having Yoda-like calm. High-functioning reflective leaders appear able to maintain a level of preternatural calm that's resistant to bad luck, failure, or even insubordination. They have mastered control of the emotions that trigger reactive behavior. When you speak to someone with this level of genuine mastery and confidence, their words may not solve your problem, but they will make you feel calmer, more capable, and less in thrall to your out-of-control feelings.

> Reflective leaders manage such calm because they have a bulletproof sense of capability and worth. It's not that they don't doubt themselves; they do it constantly. But they're so secure in who they are and why they show up that they don't take criticism, chaos, or failure as *judgment*. They're simply facts on the ground that need to be dealt with. Only insecure leaders bellow and shake the windows.

Depersonalizing verbal assaults. These leaders are also highly skilled in stepping back from an emotionally charged encounter. They understand that when they are being verbally attacked, the vitriol is almost always about the attacker, not about themselves. Instead of vomiting pent-up feelings in response, they're capable of detaching themselves from the situation, like someone watching a play. After the storm passes, they can respond calmly and with empathy and say, "Hold on, how would you feel if I said that to you? What's this really all about?"

Asking for help. Because they're humble enough to admit they *have* blind spots and have the awareness to see them, reflective leaders are more likely to surround themselves with people who help them navigate those weak areas. This also speaks to confidence and not feeling judged because they see people who are smarter and better about some things than they are as assets, not threats.

Distinguishing between empathy and accountability. Much has been written about the value of emotional intelligence, yet the dangers of too much empathy are rarely mentioned. Being able to see others' point of view is important; when you can appreciate their dreams, concerns, and goals you can connect more deeply. But too much empathy enables bad behavior and is counterproductive. It prevents leaders from holding people strictly accountable for their actions and the achievement of specific goals. Leaders, like parents, must draw clear boundaries: "I care about you, but that care does not relieve you of the obligation to meet your objectives and behave."

One of the classic examples involves the great UCLA men's basketball coach John Wooden. For years, Wooden had maintained a strict clean-shaven rule for his players. Then in 1972, after the team went undefeated and won the NCAA championship, the famously free-spirited center Bill Walton, the best player on the team, showed up for practice with a long beard and flowing hair that made him look like he'd been cast in a shampoo commercial. His attitude was simple: Coach Wooden didn't have the right to tell him how to wear his hair. When Walton said this, Wooden nodded calmly and replied, "You're right, Bill, but I do have the right to decide who will play and who won't." Walton shaved off his beard and cut his hair that day. Wooden empathized with Walton's view but still held him accountable.

When overly empathetic reactions reward continued bad habits or missed deadlines, it is corrosive to the larger organization. When someone can exploit empathy to miss KPIs or treat people without respect, the entire culture or value chain will descend to this lower denominator.

Changing or terminating relationships that don't work. They don't try to save people. It's not your job to save people or coach the uncoachable. You can't change anyone but yourself, and that's not easy either. Remember the Serenity Prayer? "God grant me the serenity to accept the things I cannot change, courage to change the things I can, and wisdom to know the difference." It should be carved on the wall of every CEO's office.

Practicing active reflection. Thinking about what just happened and why. Buddhist monk Henepola Gunaratana wrote, "Mindfulness is present moment awareness. It takes place in the here and now. It is the observance of what is happening right now, in the present. It stays forever in the present, perpetually on the crest of the ongoing wave of passing time."[5] If you can do that, I want to buy *your* book. That kind of awareness takes years to develop, if ever. Most of us have little awareness of the present moment. Our minds live either in anticipation of what *will* happen or reflection on what *already* happened. But as Eckhart Tolle wrote, "Realize deeply that the present moment is all you have. Make the now the primary focus of your life."[6] Your ability to be present and stay present is the most important ability you will ever develop.

> We don't learn from experience; we learn from reflection on our experience. It's important to practice thinking about what you did on a given day or in a certain meeting, separating your thoughts and feelings from the facts. What choices did you make and why? What could you have done differently? Were you reacting based on a program or responding thoughtfully?
>
> Whatever you practice grows stronger. One of the benefits of reflective leadership is confidence in your decision-making process. Even if you make a bad decision or get a bad outcome, you can learn and continue to lead.

Leading with humility. When it's warranted, leading with an apology is powerful. I can do this in meetings and Zoom calls, but for years, I couldn't. I thought apologies were for the weak. Far from it. Only someone with a deep well of self-esteem will willingly, happily admit to being wrong or looking foolish instead of making up reasons why they were right but bad luck got in the way. Leading with an apology is self-deprecating and disarming and a marvelous way to build trust and put people at ease around you because they now know that *you* know you're as flawed as they are.

JumpCrew's Circles are facilitated by a team member who completes a few hours of training. The training is great for facilitating peer forums and for leading any kind of meeting. However, it's by no means comprehensive training, and facilitating a deep, meaningful talk with seven or eight people who barely know each other is a big task. That's why humility is like a magic spell. When I spoke with a group of facilitators about their first meetings, a facilitator named Kristin Burton told me, "I opened the meeting by telling my Circle that I was a little bit nervous. It really broke the ice. I felt better, and people really opened up." I almost melted with appreciation at that.

Deep Dive

In 1988, Graham Gibbs developed a model he called "The Reflective Cycle." Its object was to give people a framework for examining and learning from repeated experiences, effectively helping them avoid making the same mistakes over and over. The cycle has six stages:

1. **Description.** What happened? Don't make judgments yet or try to draw conclusions; simply describe.
2. **Feelings.** What were your reactions and feelings? Don't analyze them yet, just catalog your emotions in the moment.
3. **Evaluation.** What was good or bad about the experience? Now is the time to make value judgments.

4. **Analysis.** Why did what happened happen? Put on your detective hat and recruit others to give you different perspectives. What was really going on? Why did you say or do what you did? What were other people's experiences like?

5. **Conclusion.** There are two kinds of conclusions, general and specific. First, what can you conclude from your experiences and analysis generally? How could the situation have been handled differently, and what would a better result look like? Then be specific. What about your program contributed to the outcome? What do you need to change about your response to ensure a better outcome?

6. **Action plan.** What will you do differently in this type of situation next time? What have you learned and how will you apply it?

Are You a Reflective Leader?

Bridgewater Associates is a $17 billion hedge fund, one of the most important in the world. For more than a decade, it was run by Eileen Murray, who served as co-CEO with David McCormick. Murray's challenge was to keep the intense stress and breakneck pace of the company from crushing the motivation out of its top investment managers, some of the most gifted people in the financial world. How do you get brilliant, mostly male, type A personalities accustomed to a kill-or-be-killed culture to let their guard down, be vulnerable, and talk about their fears and worries?

Well, reflective leaders model reflection for their subordinates, so Murray scheduled one-on-one coaching sessions with her top performers and began each one by talking about her own anxieties and failings. In an article in the Harvard Business Review, she described what she would often say, her description of what it was like to become the first woman to lead a major hedge fund: "You can imagine all of the fears swirling around in my head: fear of looking stupid, fear of getting fired for making a bad decision, fear of saying something that got perversely twisted in the press, fear of letting down my board of directors. I openly shared my angst with subordinates. I was an open book. Honesty is the cornerstone for all trusting relationships, and it had to start with me."[7]

Ms. Murray's brave course of action demonstrates the next step for any leader who aspires to become a reflective leader: *becoming transparent*. Transparent leaders display self-awareness, vulnerability, and candor on the job and with subordinates. As Murray said, the experience was unnerving, but she also had no other choice. You're either all in on mindfulness and accepting of your own flaws and failings, or you're not. Your employees will see half measures as half-hearted attempts to win them over with no cost to yourself—or worse, as hypocrisy. Reflective leadership takes commitment.

At JumpCrew, Rob and I try to honor that commitment even while things are rapidly shifting around us. One person who can attest to that is Jarron Vosburg, one of our VP of sales. Jarron has a rare combination of assets for a young leader—drive, talent, focus with a well of self-awareness, and a strong vision of what he wants to accomplish—and they have enabled him to rise high in the organization in a short amount of time. I asked him about how the JumpCrew culture evolved with the move to WFH and this is what he said:

"We started having all-hands meetings virtually, and that created an intimacy that we hadn't felt when we had all-hands meetings together in the office," Jarron responded. "Everyone used to be sitting in rows twenty deep, with speakers at the front of the room with a microphone and a projector. Now it feels like three hundred people are all sitting around a table. This happened right after the first weekend of a lot of the Black Lives Matter protests and rallies. It started as a meeting, going through some updates about the company, but then Rob and David opened up the floor and teed up the topic for anyone to contribute if they had something to say.

"What I found really powerful about that was two things. One, as an organization, we took on the challenging conversation," he went on. "Second, I was proud that five or ten different people, including a bunch of fairly new hires, took the opportunity to speak from their most personal and difficult experiences (being Black and American)—to share what they were going through in front of a camera with three hundred people. That told me that not only did we find great talent, but we have a community that can foster conversation in a productive way. We've created an environment where people feel comfortable sharing in a less-than-intimate setting, knowing that their CEO, chairman, leadership and their coworkers are there, completely with them.

"I was floored by how powerful of an experience it was," Jarron concluded. "I think everybody left that call feeling one notch closer to everybody within the organization. With us moving to remote work, where everyone was going through stuff in their personal lives, it felt like the unit was never tighter, despite having never having been farther apart physically. Talk about counterintuitive."

That knocks me over with pride. It's a validation of everything we tried to do, not only in moving to solitary work environments under pressure, but in laying the groundwork for a winning remote organization long before the world changed. It worked. It *works*.

Suppose that having three hundred people coming together in a virtual space and feeling as warm, intimate, and connected as family is the end point. How do you get there? Where do you start in becoming a reflective leader? These are some of the checkpoints you can begin working on to become more reflective. Consider each one a practice worth practicing.

Slow down your reactions. Respond mindfully to events and consider how others might react to your words and actions. Sometimes that requires not answering in real time, and that's okay. Understanding the impact you have on others even when you're not in the room is also especially important when you don't have the luxury of walking into someone's office to walk back a quick reaction or angry outburst.

> Being less reactive is crucial when remote work makes leadership *reputational*. Is your reputation for a considered, thoughtful response (encouraging your peers to seek you out) or for being unflinchingly judgmental (encouraging them to avoid you)? How your peers perceive you creates or limits your own room for growth. It determines how willing people are to approach you, trust you, and confide in you. If you're seen as a hothead, you become a liability to your culture and individuals in your tribe. If you're seen as a peacemaker and a sage, you're a one-person safe space.
>
> You can slow your reaction time and not lose the fast pace needed for high achievement. I went to bartending school when I was eighteen, and they taught us that the fastest way to make drinks in a packed bar isn't to move faster but to know where everything is and to move with purpose. The amateur thinks he's saving time by moving faster and may-

be scooping ice with the glass instead of taking the time to find and use the ice scooper—until he breaks the glass in the ice and has to close the bar so he can melt the ice and find the broken glass.

Mindful action is the key. Every action for a reason. Good intentions are no excuse for careless actions. You're not slow-walking decisions; you're just not making them out of irritation or impatience. You're taking a beat, understanding the forces at play, objectively seeing your own needs and those of the team and making a mindful, thoughtful call.

See yourself as others do. What does your behavior tell you about yourself? What does your team's behavior tell you about each person on it? Be in the present moment with full awareness, active listening, presence, and gratitude, rather than dwelling on the past or anticipating the future. This will help you develop the metacognition to step outside of yourself and ask, "Is Talia hearing what I'm saying?" or "Billie seems to be anxious about our plans; why and what can I do to address her discomfort?"

Presence enables you to be calming and grounding, letting you appreciate the nuance of what's happening. It also conveys genuine respect and concern for others. You're also able to be empathetic without being enabling. Aim to understand each person's state of mind and needs and still make it clear that you're holding them accountable.

Align your words and actions. Are you who you say you are? Do you do what you say you will do? Are you really the leader you say you are, or are you selling an image to feel better about yourself?

Reflective leaders are more consistent. They are clear about their intentions and back up their words with action. Their teams always know where they stand. "Do what you say you are going to" is a simple motto that Rob has championed to establish alignment across our community.

Bury ego. We tend to look for evidence that confirms our biased preexisting beliefs because that feeds our ego. Human beings love to be right. But when you ignore everything that contradicts what you believe, you're defenseless against reality. You can wind up filled with hubris and unjustified pride that leads to disaster.

> Perhaps the most famous example of this came in 1986 when engineers from the NASA contractor Morton Thiokol advised the space agency to postpone the next morning's launch of the space shuttle Challenger. The weather forecast called for temperatures as low as twenty-seven degrees Fahrenheit, and the engineers worried that the O-ring seals on the solid rocket boosters would fail in the cold, causing a possible explosion. NASA officials ignored the call for a postponement and went ahead with the launch. The result, of course, was a catastrophe that killed all seven astronauts.
>
> Being a reflective leader means understanding the seductions of the ego. We all have an ego, but leaders are rarely served by giving into the ego's need for gratification. It's like the Cherokee story of the two wolves. We all have two wolves in us. One is anger, envy, regret, greed, arrogance, guilt, resentment, lies, false pride, and ego. The other is joy, peace, love, hope, serenity, humility, kindness, generosity, truth, compassion, and faith.

Which wolf wins? *The one you feed.*

Being kind, seeking to learn and not dominate, taking risks, understanding the burdens others bear, being of service—these are health food for the ego. They boost self-esteem. Domination, intimidation, and manipulation are crack for the ego. They're addictive, but their high is temporary and empty and is never enough because the real hunger is your need for self-love and self-worth.

Be authentic. Reflective leaders don't need to put on a show. They don't care about conforming to the tired stereotypes of the traditional leader archetype: the charismatic P.T. Barnum showman, the screaming tyrant, or anal-retentive stickler for detail. They show up as who they are. They feel free to be weak or sad, talk about their troubles, or share stories from their past. They're not afraid to be human. In my experience, this is the best, fastest way to forge a deep connection with people.

Authenticity is the glue to building and maintain relationships regardless of location. It frees you of the need to maintain a façade or be strong and impregnable 100 percent of the time. Leaders can screw up, be afraid, and have an occasional barking dog or crying child in their MS Teams or Google meeting. You get to be one of the tribe. The more transparency you are able to bring your relationships, the more peace of mind you will have, and that's something in short supply for any leader.

Chapter Four

LEADING A REFLECTIVE ORGANIZATION

Freedom is not a state; it is an act. It is not some enchanted garden perched high on a distant plateau where we can finally sit down and rest. Freedom is the continuous action we all must take.

—Rep. John Lewis

In my younger days, I was fortunate enough to work under some truly authentic leaders, people gifted at building trusting relationships. Something about them made them unflappable, confident, and fully present. They were able to take a genuine, lead-forward interest in me and share their own experiences but not feel that doing so diminished them. They had a deeper understanding of and comfort level with who they were and their limits than anyone I'd ever met.

That brings me to Eugene Greene. Eugene was one of the most generous and compassionate entrepreneurs I have known and the best, most authentic salesman I have ever met. When we met, I had already produced a feature film and had moved onto working for a tyrannical Hollywood producer. He convinced me to give up the glitz and glamour of L.A. and move back to New York for an entry-level sales job selling temporary help to office managers. That was a hard, big deal to close.

One Friday afternoon, he and I were coming back from sales calls, and there was a long line out the office door. The company employed hundreds of temps, and they were waiting for their paychecks. These were people's food and rent checks, so getting them right was critical. But one guy's check had been wrong, and he was angry. When I saw this young hothead creating a scene in the lobby, I got scared and hid in my office. Finally, I crept back to the lobby and asked where the guy was, and the receptionist told me, "He's in Eugene's office."

Eugene's office? This couldn't be good. I hustled to my boss's office, and there Eugene was with his arm around the guy, bonding over his collection of New York Knicks memorabilia. This man had been having a panic attack because he didn't think he was going to be able to pay his rent, and Eugene connected with him like he would his own son. He had an amazing way of engaging with people by being a decent, real, warm-hearted man. That really showed me the difference between how I handled people and how you could handle them if you were focused on their needs, like Eugene was.

Leaders like Eugene make you want to leave everything you have on the field for them. I *wanted* him to be proud of me. The Eugenes of the world don't need to give Tony Robbins-style speeches to motivate their team. They make you feel a part of something greater than yourself and make you want to give your best, stay late, and achieve more.

For the better part of my twenties, I looked to see that kind of leader in the mirror and didn't. I wanted to be enthusiastic and confident, but I was blind to the need for focus, discipline, patience, and mastery. For years, I looked for a mentor, someone who would recognize my talent and show me the way. But I was on the wrong search. The real work was to look inside and become the leader I was searching for. For that, there is no shortcut; it's a lifetime of work.

In an organization, the most common hurdle for the reactive leader is the failure to see the negative impact of their behavior on their own progress and other people's experience. It could be an emotional outburst, lack of preparation, an inability to listen or just the overconfidence, but however that lack of self-awareness and mindfulness manifests, it's toxic to any organization and its people.

The most visible sign of this is the leader who appears to be "out over their skis," meaning beyond even their discomfort zone. Reactive leaders are also more prone to blaming others and themselves for events out of anyone's control. The signals are more easily overlooked during boom times but impossible to miss when things go south and fingers start pointing. But it's during the hard times when organizations face difficult decisions that reflective leaders are needed the most. Layoffs, furloughs, pay reductions, and turnover can break an organization or bring it together. Handled well, such challenges can make it a stronger community of people with a shared understanding working toward shared goals.

The outcome depends on the leadership. You'll do hard things that won't make everyone happy. Accept it and keep moving. How you handle business when it's not pretty is what qualifies you to lead. Lean into the least desirable moments. Without that, you're following, not leading.

That brings us to the WFH world. It's my purpose to look at leadership through the same lens that John Lewis saw freedom: a never-ending process of personal development and conscious growth. Nowhere is the need for that more apparent than in the work-from-home organization, where feedback must be earned and it's easy for leaders to lose contact with their communities.

It does matter. Because everything leaders do affects the most distant corners of the organization and everyone in them. Reflective leadership is the linchpin of a successful, growing WFH team and organization. It provides the best opportunity for people to grow into their roles, thrive individually, improve execution, and accelerate achievement. Let's find out how.

How Reflective Leaders Make a Positive Difference

I got to know Dr. Brad Reedy from listening to his great podcast *Evoke* and was immediately impressed with the depth of his thinking and the humanity of his presence. Brad has a PhD in marriage and family therapy; is the co-owner and clinical director of Evoke Therapy Programs, which provides outdoor-based therapy for adolescents, young adults, and families; and is the author of the wonderful *The Journey of the Heroic Parent: Your Child's Struggle &*

the Road Home. I spoke with him for this book, and I asked him about the responsibility of a leader to put in the work. His answer really highlighted for me the impact that a leader can have on the health of an organization.

"The idea of organizational health is based on this idea that our partners, leaders, and managers are all going to do their own work," he said. "Otherwise . . . you're protecting your ego. You're protecting an image. You're feeling insecure and threatened. All the things that would happen in the context of being a parent that also create a liability for you as a leader.

"Leaders need to get to a place where we can own our stuff, acknowledge it, apologize, and then move on," he continues. "Organizational health means that we all do our own work and nobody is excluded from critique. If I'm supervising a therapist, and my insecurity or ego comes into play, my team is going to call me on it in front of everybody else. I'll say I made a mistake, or I was being reactive, or I was feeling scared, or I was feeling upset—whatever I need to do to be real and present. Organizational health means leaders are constantly leaning into their fallibility, modeling their willingness to admit mistakes and apologize."

That's the first and most basic way reflective leaders change an organization: *modeling desirable behavior.* The superficial indicators of leadership are meaningless in the WFH world. The parking space, corner office, the Tesla . . . nobody cares when you're at home. While the principles of leadership might be the same whether you're working in a face-to-face org or a remote one, the *expression* of leadership is very different.

The tools that used to convey authority and power—voice, attire, posture, presence, being at the front of the room, order of speaking—are worthless. Now leading is about who you are and the things you do to demonstrate your values and priorities. Leaders are exposed in the WFH world. What you model becomes part of the DNA of the community.

Writing for the *Harvard Business Review*, former Red Hat CEO Jim Whitehurst says that the behavior of leaders, not how they get others to behave, is what shapes a company's culture. "Picture the following scenario," he writes. "A group of executives decide that their organizational culture needs to become more 'customer focused.' But when you look at the agenda of their meetings, there's no time devoted to discussing how they can improve their customers' experience. And how much time do those executives actually spend out in the field, visiting customers, let alone fielding calls from them? If these executives prioritize something other than customers in their behavior, don't you think the rest of the organization will follow suit?"[1]

It's the same in a WFH organization as in any traditional organization. Leaders lead by going first, by demonstrating the behavior we want to see from others. Want your teams to communicate about the bad things customers are saying? Communicate clearly and transparently with them. Want your team to be calm and collected under stress? Exhibit those qualities yourself to excess. Want your teams to be like family? Treat everyone, from your peers to new hires, with warmth and personal attention. Remember, you get the wolf you feed.

Modeling is, quite simply, walking the talk. It's showing up daily, embodying the qualities you want to see throughout your team or community. You're not overtly teaching anyone how to act; you're demonstrating the benefit of proactivity, gratitude, humility, humor, kindness, or communication and counting on everyone else to notice. They will. You're leading. Everything flows downstream from you.

Strong Relationships

It's much easier to build and maintain relationships with people when you share the same space five days a week. In 2019 at JumpCrew, we would regularly have team and company outings. Happy hour, bowling night, or a night on Broadway in Nashville brought shared excitement and opportunities to bond. Then in 2020, we had hundreds of people gathering in small online Circles. They would meet in groups of seven or eight, mostly with people they didn't know from other teams, and one designated facilitator. The participants would share an article about the meeting's theme—vulnerability, collaboration, what work from home was like—peppering in personal experiences and helping solve each other's problems. That's how you build relationships when you can't be in the same office. It's harder, but it can happen. Small talk was replaced with "big talk" and enabled a much deeper experience and connection than any virtual happy hour ever could.

But it can only happen when you as the leader or the facilitator create the safe space for openness and sharing without shame or fear of being judged. We all fear that others will see our experiences, judge us, and find us lacking in some way. Here's an example of what I mean, though it came before JumpCrew was forced to go all virtual.

I was holding a meeting for our new managers, maybe ten or twelve of us in the room. I was trying to get the people in the room to open up, so after a "get to know you" warm-up failed at getting people to talk about how they were feeling, I decided to share more deeply about what was going on in my personal life, highlighting some of my own journey and struggles. Leaders go first. Two years into my second marriage, I was getting divorced, I told the group. The veneer of my "perfect family" life had cracked. Now my twelve-year-old daughter, who'd adjusted to nuclear family life eight years after her mother died, was in a panic, and my two stepchildren, both sixteen, were angry with me. Needless to say, this wasn't the story the room had expected from a leadership workshop.

Then I asked people to engage and share their own stories, initially the others mostly sat staring at each other uncomfortably. However, my prior experiences in these new leader workshops had been similar: after I had shared personal stories, others became willing to go deep, so I decided to let the silence linger a bit. Still, silence. Then, I decided to push a little. I noticed that one guy in the room had been promoted to team lead in one of our more volatile divisions. We pushed our teams to sell hard, and their product had been having issues for months, yet in the sea of turmoil, he always maintained his calm. Now I asked him why that was.

The first two times I asked how he did it, he dodged the question and said he didn't know. But I kept pressing. Finally, the third time I asked, he said, "I was homeless as a kid."

Dead silence.

I gave it a few beats to sink in and said, "Thank you for sharing that. I really appreciate it." Talk about programs that impact your future. Something had given this young man the resilience and self-awareness to lead a challenging team, and I knew that made him special. I did not know where his motivation or approach came from, but he had something different. Being homeless as a child had done that.

In that instant, all of us in the room became connected. His courage and honesty took down the walls and pretenses. There was trust and confidence, and not just between me and that colleague. Everyone else was watching how I shared and brought out and received this guy's story. If he had thought I was a jerk for pushing him, or if he didn't trust that I would treat his story with respect, he wouldn't have shared it, or sharing it would have backfired. The funny thing was, I wasn't specifically trying to create a connection with him. I was trying to plant the seed of a relationship between twelve people. Well, once he shared, the floodgates opened. Everyone had to share something. Bonds formed. Community formed.

The reflective leader is the custodian of relationships in the organization, the traffic cop. Relationships can exist without you being a part of them, of course, but you till the soil in which those relationships take root. You set the thermostat for trust, respect, and the importance everyone places on each other's personal lives. I was custodian of that young man's story, a safe landing place for vulnerability. Once I showed them that sharing and openness were to be highly regarded, everyone else took the cue.

In WFH, the role of the leader is more challenging, intentional, and magnified. It's easy and tempting to cocoon. You have to draw people out of their shell and give them reasons to engage. If anything, the need for connection and warm, family-like relationships is even greater. Think of yourself as a safe space, a soft place for everyone to land. What kind of work should you do to be that boss? For me, in order to be truly open and welcoming to everyone else's story, I had to find peace with my own. Start there.

Trust

Lavall Chichester was JumpCrew's chief marketing officer through the formative period of our culture, and he's a super interesting guy. He grew up in Brooklyn, went to Brooklyn Tech, was a break-dancer back in the day, and then moved on to become a mixed martial arts fighter. Somewhere, there's a YouTube video of him launching a crazy roundhouse kick two seconds into a fight and just smashing some poor guy's nose. But he's also wonderfully emotional and the sweetest, gentlest guy you'd ever meet in your life, which leads me to my point.

In WFH, you can't just go where the water flows. You have to push against inertia and live with tension. When Rob hired Lavall for JumpCrew, he had never led the marketing arm of a three hundred-person company. But he demonstrated an amazing ability to adapt himself to the environment, particularly when the company needs grew faster than his skillset and especially after the WFH move. So he was able to refine his role always find ways to contribute.

Lavall is reflective, and he's adaptable. Adaptability means having a fluid sense of self. If you're a leader, and you define yourself as just one thing—a badass negotiator, a problem solver, a visionary—you'll cling to that identity and protect it. We are all programmed to protect our existing identity. However, when you're reflective and self-aware, you can adapt because no single thing defines you. Work doesn't need to be about you. That's why Lavall is a terrific leader, especially for a WFH company. He's secure in his identity, so he can adapt to the needs of his team, and that's why reflective leaders are so good at building trust.

"The only way this works is if you trust that you've hired people who are just going to do their job, not gonna slink off and be unreliable," he says. "But you need to find those people and weed them out. The old hypothesis at JumpCrew was 'There's no work from home because people will not do their job.' Now, we've changed the culture. It's less suspicious and more like, 'Okay, cool. Let's get this done right unless it's blatantly obvious that someone's doing something they shouldn't.' Once you have that paradigm, that shift in mindset, you start trusting in other areas that maybe you didn't trust before. You continue to build that trust by setting expectations and watching people meet them or not. That has brought us together. The trust level has increased for sure. This has been a crucible."

Morale, loyalty, mutual support—they all hinge on trust. Your team has to believe that you put their needs on an even par with your own needs and those of the organization, that you *care* about them. That's something you have to prove and keep proving, especially in WFH, where overtures to employee's personal lives aren't as easy or obvious. Talk is cheap, and trust is risky. You can get burned. But what is the alternative?

Productivity

There's a belief that productivity begins and ends with tools and processes, and to a degree, that's true. JumpCrew is a sales organization, and with everyone moving to WFH, we were trusting our reps and everybody else to work independently and maintain their level of productivity—to hit their numbers without real-time feedback. That's a big ask. For the leader, success depends a great deal on what behavioral economist and psychologist Daniel Kahneman identified in his book *Thinking Fast and Slow* as System One and System Two thinking.[2]

Simply put, the mind toggles back and forth between these two systems. System One is intuitive reasoning, reaching conclusions based on "gut feeling." System Two is analytical reasoning based on evidence and logical judgment. While most leaders trained and mentored in traditional leadership probably have more well-developed System Two processes, that can leave them in the cold when it comes to dealing with unpredictable circumstances like, say, everyone suddenly decamping to work in their kitchens.

Like most organizations before WFH, JumpCrew started out being more System Two than System One in thinking. For us, that meant data and tools. After all, if you're thinking is based purely on logic, giving salespeople more data and more productivity tools should equal more productivity even if they're working from home instead in a raucous sales bullpen, right?

Once we went to WFH, we started using technology to hyper connect our sales reps to everything that was going on, including their real-time sales metrics. They weren't sitting at home, twiddling their thumbs, wondering, "What's happening?" We had a wealth of data inside JumpCrew on activity, phone calls, conversion metrics, opportunities, and we were just sitting on it. So we figured out how we could make that data work for us, using informed decisions to help guide us on Salesforce and actually get deals closed. Now, if you're a sales rep, you can see all of your leads and opportunities. If you're a manager, you can watch the KPIs for each of your respective teams. The next step is that this starts to become adaptively intelligent, which means that based on the data in certain time periods during the day, week, or month, and based on the way the reps are working, the tool makes recommendations in a real-time recommendation feed or through push notifications.

That's all great, but it's all System Two, pure logic. These are also human beings. So while our salespeople making their numbers is critical to our survival as an organization, we also have to create other System One metrics based on our intuition and feelings. Salespeople in particular tend to be gregarious, social animals, and now they're alone with themselves all day lacking that social energy they feed on. We had to see that, recognize it as important, and take action. So we started reaching out more often and letting them know that their mental health and well-being are just as important as their numbers.

How happy are they? How engaged? How social and relaxed at online meetings? Yes, none of that matters in the end if they fail to hit their numbers and generate revenue, but attending to those soft metrics is what *enables* them to hit their numbers. Too many leaders are enamored of hard data and metrics that can be laid out on a spreadsheet, but people aren't columns of numbers. Safety, satisfaction, the sense of been heard and seen, a feeling of belonging—these are just as crucial to profitability as quarterly sales figures.

Communication

In *Dare to Lead*, Brené Brown writes, "Clear is kind. Unclear is unkind."[3] Clarity in communication doesn't just prevent misunderstandings and fear. It also tells your people, "I trust your maturity and wisdom enough to give you all the facts." By being clear, you empower people to respond to the circumstances without needing to interpret them—to step up and meet the moment, to distinguish between an ask and a requirement, and to do it all without needing to read your mind.

For the reflective leader in a WFH world, communication is also a matter of what subjects you choose to allow into your culture. You're the gatekeeper; what you make a priority for yourself becomes a priority for everyone. The reality is, personal or sensitive subjects, from politics to scandal to the company's future, will always come up. So be clear about what's acceptable and what's not. If you value and demand "no gossip" in the organization, then be clear about it and shut down the noncompliant. Otherwise, be prepared for distractions based on a lack of clarity because gossip will become part of the larger conversation.

At JumpCrew, we chose to lean into deeper topics that might make you squirm. The sense that "we're all in this together" is powerful glue for the community, and that comes in part through sharing stories, each person's truth or their reaction to the day's events. Why do you think indigenous tribes sat in a circle around a fire telling stories? We have done that with big events like COVID and Black Lives Matter but also with more mundane details of people's lives and histories that we share in Circles. And we soon saw there was nothing to be afraid of.

If only other companies felt the same way. But a 2019 survey conducted by *Chief Executive* and the USC Annenberg Center for Public Relations found that 44 percent of CEOs said their most important communication goal was sales, and their second most important goal was brand differentiation.[4] While we suspect that the world-shaking events of 2020 might have shifted those numbers a bit, it's a sure bet that many orgs will continue to duck uncomfortable, personal topics. That's a mistake. In WFH, ignoring the things people feel strongly about only increases their sense of isolation.

By the way, as the leader, your style of communication is contagious. You are visible when you are talking and also when you are listening. Listening attentively, being comfortable with silence, calm, slowing conversation down so it becomes an exchange and not competition to see who can get the last word—those will set the tone for a more reflective culture.

Accountability and Motivation

Accountability is my personal first commandment. Be accountable for what you say you'll do with no excuses. Leaders in a great remote organization have to be driven, demand excellence, and hold everyone accountable for showing up at their best every day. There is no other way to create and maintain a culture of accelerated achievement. That said, leaders, just like everyone else, *are* flawed and vulnerable. Refusing to admit that you screwed up sometimes doesn't make your people think you're Superman; it tells them you're either too egotistical, insecure, or blind to your own weaknesses.

But how do you walk that tightrope as a reflective leader? How do you express authenticity and let people know it's okay not to be perfect while still setting high expectations and holding people to them?

First, you absolutely *must* hold yourself to a higher standard of accountability than your team. Don't beat your chest, don't talk about it, just do it—stay late, get the job done, close the deal, beat the deadline. Demonstrate mastery. Be the example. Be accountable to everyone, even the lowest person on the totem pole. But just as important is this idea:

. . . .

It's not your job to save anyone.

. . . .

You'll make sure your team has everything they need to excel and enjoy the process and struggle to accelerate achievement: training, mentoring, technology, candid feedback, coaching, peers who care, the right comp plans and products they can believe in. But in return, you want their best. You demand and *expect* it. Say that clearly, and say it often.

Earlier in my career, I tended to err on the side of, "Hey, let's stay with this guy. He just needs more support. One more month.

More one-on-ones." That's okay to a point, but there also comes a time when people must move beyond handholding, step up, and deliver on expectations. Achieving this balance between offering support and insisting on accountability and results is one of the great challenges of WFH. What is the combination of quantitative and qualitative indicators that tell a manager that a rep is underperforming? And what do we do about that?

Well, in this strange world, until new norms harden, we give everyone a little more rope, a little more time to adapt. You probably need it, too. So you slow your reactions and use your empathy to put yourself in the other person's shoes. But when you cross over into making excuses, it's over.

As I said before, in the WFH world, the reflective leader's job is to till the ground for planting a culture in which a world-class remote company can grow. You are supporting and empowering people, and enabling one to consistently miss his numbers and stay employed will enable others to do the same. You're building trust, fostering communication, letting people solve their own problems, tending the soil with healthy amounts of vulnerability and shared humanity. You are creating the fertile ground. But you are also saying to each employee, "All right, it's time to step to the plate and show that you can come through for the team." There is nothing wrong with doing that. Results matter.

Each person's journey is different. Some will be ready for the challenge when you want them to be, and some will still be learning. By its nature, a remote organization that values growth, achievement, and accountability is more demanding than most and has higher turnover because of it. Every person JumpCrew has ever hired has heard me talk about confidence and potential. We believe each person we hire has the ability to be great, and we believe they can find their "great" in the roles we hire them for. If we discover that we were wrong, we aren't helping that person find his or her greatness by keeping them in a role that doesn't suit them, and we let them know. Our new hires know that if they discover for whatever reason that this is not an environment they can be great in, they should speak up. No harm, no foul. If someone can't do the job well, cutting them loose is a favor to the organization and to the individual.

Morale

Design thinking practices (what's possible vs. what's probable) are another way of looking at the methods most effective for communicating the plan, calibrating risk, course correcting, offering praise, and insisting on results. Stanford University's Institute popularized design thinking as a way to "understand customers by challenging assumptions and refining the problems in an iterative process."

I like this approach because it enables you to examine a problem from all sides and reframe it to come up with novel solutions. I also like it because it encourages the entire organization to view situations in terms of finding solutions, not blame. That's great for morale. Everyone likes to feel as though everyone in the org is subject to the same rules.

Self-awareness and emotional intelligence are key in creating a culture where constructive criticism, even and *especially* of the boss, is welcome and encouraged. When people feel empowered to disagree and offer their different opinion—they feel empowered.

Stop and consider how you call meetings, send messages, and speak to people and why you make those particular choices. One Friday evening at around eight o'clock, I was reminded of that. One of my managers sent out a terribly worded group email, and I was so triggered by its awkward callousness that I began to dash off an angry rebuke, which would have been seen by the entire team. Then I stopped myself. Lashing out mindlessly at one of our managers just as he was settling into a weekend with his kids wouldn't set an example of reflective leadership; it would create anxiety and tension for someone else all weekend. I saved the email and sent it on Monday, and I'm glad I did.

Examine your actions, and understand if they serve the ultimate goal of the reflective leader: inspiring others to show up as their best selves as often as possible. The smallest actions and interactions of senior leaders carry great meaning. Fill your interactions with care and self-awareness. This doesn't imply a large shift in thinking or action. Think about micro-adjustments the way a golfer or tennis player does. Sometimes, a small tweak produces radical improvement results. Sometimes, a small tweak to how you're thinking about a person or a problem dramatically changes the outcome.

Look at these two different ways a leader might counsel a subordinate with a problem:

- Empowering: "What do you think?" or "How do you see it?"
- Neutering: "Let me tell you what I would do . . ."

Everyone knows you're in charge. You don't have to act like it. When everyone feels there's a level playing field where all can speak their mind and be respected and where even the leaders have to play by the same rules, morale soars.

Deep Dive
THE WEST WING RULE

In a WFH world, walking chats in the hallways (made famous in the TV show *The West Wing*) are dead. Interaction is intentional. It should be scheduled and multimodal—frequent enough that it helps people feel connected and cared about, infrequent enough that it protects autonomy, doesn't make them feel surveilled, and doesn't disrupt work. Think Zoom, but also Slack, Microsoft Teams, Circl.es, and even—gasp!—talking on the phone.

Reflective Leadership on the Ground

So there's this tool, created way back in 1955 by Joe Luft and Harry Ingham, that provides a clear, simple way to understand the challenge of being a reflective leader. It's called the Johari Window, and it looks like this:

The Johari Window illustrates the four areas in which your self-awareness and other people's awareness of you intersect. In the **Arena**, you and another person both know things about you, ranging from the clothes you prefer to wear to how you handle conflict. In the **Façade** reside the things you know about yourself but another person doesn't know. In the **Blind Spot**, we find the traits and patterns that others see but you don't know about or acknowledge. And the surprises, the traits no one knows about, live in the **Unknown**. As you can imagine, my greatest concern is with the Blind Spot.

The tendencies or programs you don't know about—or worse,

that you deny—are the true saboteurs of your journey to reflective leadership. If you're passive-aggressive or uncommunicative and everyone sees that but you, it won't be long before everyone you lead is either cowering in fear or leaving the company. Blind spots are dangerous because you're unaware of behaviors that might be creating fear, uncertainty, or resentment. That's an especially acute problem in a WFH org because there's no immediate feedback mechanism—an angry employee, a meeting that falls apart—to warn you when you've stepped over a line.

The journey to becoming reflective is about eliminating your blind spots, becoming fully aware not only of who you are but what others see in you. That's challenging enough on your own when you have the time and space to reflect on your past, ask hard questions, and examine the consequences of your words and actions. It's orders of magnitude tougher when you're also trying to run a company. You don't have the luxury of retreating to a mountaintop; you have to hire, manage departments, and achieve profitability. You have to fast track reflectiveness at work while working more deliberately away from work. That's what the remainder of this chapter will be about: reflective leadership in the real world while running a WFH organization.

What, So What, Now What

One of the keys to practicing real-time reflective leadership is having a tool or framework you can use to direct your attention to where it needs to be: on your words and actions. One of my favorite tools for that comes from a 1970 book by a teacher named Terry Borton, *Reach, Touch and Teach*. In this book, he developed a tool called "What, So What, Now What" that he intended as a thought sequence for reflective education. But it also works wonderfully for reflective leadership.

The framework is a cycle, a constant internal flow designed to help you pause in the midst of the daily demands of management, see your choices and behavior, and assess both its effect and your best responses. Because that's the greatest challenge we all face: catching our counterproductive words or actions while we still have a chance to understand their impact and make better choices. Being reflective in the sometimes-maddening flow of a busy work-day seems impossible, and it is if you believe that doing so means dropping what you're doing and sitting in the dark in lotus position. It doesn't. It's simply a framework for attention and reflection you can use anytime.

WHAT

This is simple self-reporting. You look at a task, event, or experience and acknowledge what went down. I suggest starting with simple questions like these (you can write down your answers, but it's not mandatory):

- What happened?
- What did I do?
- Why did I do it?
- Who else was involved, and what did they do?
- How did I react to other people's actions?

SO WHAT

Now, you're analyzing what happened and considering what you might have done differently. About this Borton writes, "The So

What stage is rational, intellectual, cognitive—a delving into the meaning of what has just happened." Possible questions:

- What was I feeling during the task, event, or experience?
- How did those feelings influence my words or actions?
- What were the effects of my words or actions?
- Did the situation provide me with any real-time feedback that I overlooked?
- What was the outcome, and was it optimal?

NOW WHAT

This is about what you're going to do next. You have to think about the consequences of how you handled the situation and what you'll do to make things better next time. Some questions:

- What alternative words or actions could I have chosen and why?
- What could I have chosen *not* to do or say?
- What could I do to create a different, better outcome?
- What should I *not* do?
- What help do I need to turn this reflection into a different action?
- What lesson(s) can I take away from this?

In the beginning, using Borton's tool might feel clunky, like you're taking a test in school. But with repetition, it will become easier and more fluid until you can walk through the questions and answers in your mind in minutes. It's a terrific mental framework for exposing and correcting those blind spots I talked about earlier.

Real-Time Reflectiveness

Here are some of the best practices Rob and I have found ourselves relying on as we've navigated JumpCrew through the WFH transition and kept the company growing and, somehow, thriving. Note that these are all techniques you can apply on the job, in a F2F environment or in a remote workplace. You'll still need to do your own work, but when you come down from the mountaintop, try some of what's here.

Question your approach to everything. Begin with this, every day if it's helpful. Question how you typically approach Zoom meetings, one-on-one sessions, communication, sharing personal information, resolving conflict—*everything*. You're basically reviewing the source code of your programs of origin and trying to identify patterns that get you in trouble. For example, like many leaders, my program was to be the chief problem solver and tell people, "Do it that way." The more I engaged with different parts of JumpCrew, the more Rob, as CEO, would have to undo my proposed solution. You can't solve the whole problem if you only see part of it, and my narrow view of operations often limited me. I would create conflict by not letting the manager own the solution independently or by working through communication channels that involved him.

> It took me a while, and I broke some glasses in the ice, but I've changed that pattern. Now I'm more likely to actively listen, ask probing questions, share my experience, and allow people to find their own way.

Set up accountability systems for yourself. Driving your team or organization to accelerated achievement requires focus, discipline, and, of course, accountability. At JumpCrew, we have to be accountable. We often set high expectations with clients that leave us microscopic margins for error. Results are there for everyone to see in dollars and cents. But accountability is more an attitude than a process. It can't be all about blame or punishment; it has to be about incentivizing beneficial activity. Take this example from Jarron, who spoke with me about our software to make leading a WFH sales team more fluid than when sales reps are in-house:

> It's evolved into a tool to help streamline sales, reps, activities, and communication. When our reps were working remote, our assumption was that not everybody knows how to read into a report in Salesforce. Not everybody knows how to interpret their pipeline and act on it. Not everybody knows where they stand on the leaderboard. So we said, "Let's just have one dedicated piece of technology that all of JumpCrew can use, where we can see all our salespeople living and breathing inside of this piece of technology and help encourage more community for our remote sales force." But we realized that there is a much broader application of what this tool could ultimately be.

Before, you had your sales manager sitting around with your teams, sharing real-time feedback, but now we need to get that revenue in a work from home situation. We're trusting everybody to work independently and maintain a level of productivity, to hit their numbers without that real-time feedback. So this is going to be an adaptive, intelligent tool that acts as a sales manager to guide a salesperson's activities based on the data within their pipeline. We have this wealth of data inside JumpCrew from phone calls to conversion metrics to opportunities and everywhere in between, and we're making that data work for us to create a sort of coach, using informed decisions through data to help guide our sales force and actually get deals closed.

> That's remarkable stuff, and even though in this instance it's about sales reps, the underlying principles are the same. Build an engine that can influence aspirational behavioral change and limit the less healthy, desperate motivation a salesperson feels when they are at the bottom of the stack ranking. Create systems for real-time (or, at least, timely) feedback and make them about encouraging positive behaviors instead of provoking remorse or shame for negative ones.
>
> For reflective leaders in real time, that could mean giving your peers permission to give you candid feedback in private. Or maybe what was once a quick private meeting may now start in Slack or Teams, allowing employees to nudge you when you're out of line or comment on how you're doing during meetings. That last one takes a lot of bravery, but employees appreciate and respect when leaders are transparent about trying to become better people.

Build a culture where it's safe to get personal. Many organizations that have adapted well to the changing work environment share a counterintuitive trait. Like JumpCrew, they have planted the seeds of a company culture where people's personal lives are not only respected, but people feel comfortable sharing their doubts and fears. That extends to talking about our external and internal obstacles, our thoughts and our feelings.

I know that in many organizations the personal is seen as taboo or an imposition on business, but people's personal lives don't stop being important to them the moment they walk through your door—and now they're not walking through your door at all. In the WFH world, not only are some employees facing greater levels of stress, anxiety, and isolation than before, but you're on their turf, looking into their homes, seeing their kids and pets, and hearing the sounds of the household. That's personal stuff, so get comfortable with it.

Grow a cultural fabric where sharing personal information isn't just okay but welcomed and honored, and lead by example. Try starting your morning meeting with the intention of getting everyone engaged. One of my favorite meeting warm-ups is to give people sixty seconds each to talk about their internal "weather report", how they are feeling and why. Go first. Be the first one to talk about your mood, a challenge you're dealing with, or something you feel sad about. It will be good for you and for your team.

Establish a "wisdom channel." Candid feedback and peers willing to share their experiences are essential, and in a WFH organization, community probably can't exist without them. It's tough to experience real, lasting growth without regular, compassionate, candid feedback because, like it or not, you're trapped in your own subjective perception of your words and actions. You're inclined to think you were right even when you were an asshole. Having ready access to mentors, peers, and others who will listen attentively and share their opinions is invaluable. It could be through a quick call or text, via a peer learning platform like Circl.es, or some other means.

But getting legit, "This is what happened, how did I do?" perspective from smart, thoughtful colleagues is a terrific tool to keep you humble and help you course correct.

Connect in any way possible. There's another name for the patterns I've been talking about, the decisions and actions we repeat that get us in trouble, cause friction in relationships and don't move the ball forward. *Addictions.* What else is an addiction but a compulsive behavior that's harmful but one we have no control over? Conflict avoidance, passive-aggressive behavior, indulgent empathy, a hair-trigger temper—they're all potentially addictive. But addiction is isolating, especially in WFH. When you're stuck in that loop, you feel alone. You feel unwanted or unworthy of being healed, of anyone else saying, "You know what? It's cool. Everybody messes up sometimes."

> As you're working to create an emotionally safe culture and change your own behavior to become more reflective, take every chance you can to connect with people at work. Reach out when you're thinking about it, initiate a group conversation, participate in peer forums like Circl.es, and get into lively exchanges on Slack. See people in person if you can. Make conversations about more than business and KPIs; share personal things, talk about sports, tell jokes, tease each other.

Stop trying to solve everyone's problem. Shortly, we're going to move into the section of the book on coaching culture and mindset. One of the hallmarks of a coaching culture is to recognize the value to not being the problem solver. Great coaches share insight and experience while empowering their people to find their own solutions. That's a great way to become more reflective.

> Suppress your impulse to give advice or be the hero. That infantilizes your team and fosters dependency. Instead, ask open-ended questions and make it clear they have your permission to take risks, break stuff, and fail on the way to locating the fix for what ails. Be "actively passive"—caring about the outcome but choosing to allow people to find their own way instead of being led by you.

Listen more, talk less. Needing to be the source of all direction and guidance is another sign of a dominant ego—not a good thing for a reflective leader. This is something you can do today: when you have the urge to talk (or worse, lecture), trying starting with "What do you think?" Invite others, especially subordinates, to share their opinions and ideas. Listen actively, not just waiting for your turn to speak. And if you really want to impress your people and win their hearts, ask them probing questions about their ideas and take notes.

Ask permission. Finally, asking someone's permission before you share your opinion or give them advice is a powerful tool. Saying, "Would you mind if I shared a thought about the project?" shows that you're humble, displays respect for the other person, and gives that person power. Someone is much more likely to accept your feedback if you give them a choice. But if they say, "No thank you, not right now," remember to walk away graciously.

Chapter Five

PILLAR NUMBER TWO: COACHING MINDSET AND CULTURE

Last chapter, I mentioned how in the past, JumpCrew CEO Rob Henderson regularly had to clean up the broken glass after someone told him, "David told me to do it this way." In my own defense, most of the time the problem wasn't that the employee had done what I suggested but that they hadn't been given the chance to ask their manager for guidance or figure it out themselves. So when conflicts popped up, Rob had to mend and resolve.

But the real issue was that when I said, "Do it this way," I violated the second Pillar: *A coaching mindset and culture.* What does that mean? A coaching culture is one in which leaders lead by example, working to embody the values they want their subordinates to display on the job instead of telling them what to do or how to do it. They encourage healthy, positive behavior by building *connections of influence* based on trust and the employee's belief—certainty, really—that the leader wants only what is best for them.

A coaching culture thrives on clarity and honest feedback. Leader/coaches are not only reflective but have the skill and compassion to offer even criticism in a way that doesn't bruise the ego or shame the other person. It challenges that person to find a new gear and rise to the occasion.

A coaching culture encourages but doesn't enable. Its leaders don't let people off the hook for their poor choices or errors by doing the work for them; instead, they inform and redirect and put those same people back on a path to success and self-reliance. Its leaders are willing and ready to say "I don't know" when confronted with a question that stumps them, and then they and the person asking it seek the answer together. It's a culture where questions are more important, and more welcome, than answers.

Finally, a coaching culture is one where the leader is okay with surrendering control. Leaders in this context tend to be what Matthew Dixon and Brent Adamson, authors of *The Challenger Sale*, call "challengers." We look for challengers in our hiring process. The concept of the challenger is a bedrock aspect of JumpCrew culture and a key to our onboarding. In sales, challengers are assertive people who don't just form relationships with customers; they challenge them to see their businesses in new ways.[1] This is where I had struggled in the past. I thought it was my job to give advice and tell people how to do things. In the beginning of a leader's journey, it feels good to be the one with all the answers. When you excel at making individual contributions, it's easy to think you can continue to advance when you solve someone else's problem yourself.

Well, you can't, and thinking you can is not a solution. I didn't always understand that I was sacrificing someone else's ability to grow their capacity. The leader's challenge is to decide when it's time to stop coaching and just push the other person up the hill. Your ability to do that successfully is dependent on the relationship, trust, and connection you have created. A common fear entrepreneurial leaders need to overcome is "If I loosen my iron grip on the company, we will fail." When you're an aggressive problem solver, it's easy to overlook other people's need to take the heat, rise to the occasion, turn a loss into a win, and advance in their own journey.

In a professional environment, how long can you accept behavior if the outcome isn't what you need it to be? How long before you have to step in and give direction? Laying back and waiting for the other person to find the answer contradicts the very nature of being a challenger. I once asked a new JumpCrew director if she were to take the lead on a project, how she would accomplish the task. It seemed like the right way to tap into her inner challenger and gauge her level of intrinsic motivation, but that's not how she heard my question. She wasn't yet comfortable getting outside of her comfort zone in the new work environment, and she met my words with strong resistance. I had failed to invest in the relationship and establish trust before I challenged her—and she either didn't want the challenge or wasn't ready for it. This was ultimately a setback in my ability to help her advance, but I would take the same risk again. If accelerated achievement was easy to foster, fewer organizations would struggle with mediocrity. It's not easy, and it's not without risk.

On the heels of that learning experience, I was coaching a very talented general manager for a company I acquired in 2019. New to the GM role, he was reticent to alter his operations process and manage cultural change that required him to fire long-term employees. But his most serious blind spot was a failure to act decisively on the data that showed negative trends in his business.

His confidence boosted by an inexplicable COVID-19 revenue bump, he was slow to act on the data that showed the company's traffic—the ultimate driver of revenue—trending downward. I coached and coached and coached him for three months, trying to instill the premise of reflective leadership because I desperately wanted him to act on his own initiative. I hoped that he would climb out of his hole before I had to consciously shift from coaching to problem-solving. It was excruciating to watch the division's profitability vanish under a sea of red.

In the fourth month, I switched gears and began actively managing the decision process with him. Fortunately, through this period of patience, he had come to respect my advice as I shifted from coaching to problem-solving, and our relationship remained strong, trusting and positive. I could have mandated the change earlier in the process, but I believe our relationship and the company ultimately profited from period which I chose to be more patient and allow him to grow on his own. In the end, he has been able to reflect on this experience, learn from it, appreciate it, and, most importantly, less likely to repeat it.

Reflective leaders naturally transition into being coaches because coaching requires the mentality of servant leadership that I talked about earlier: the personal mandate that you measure your own success according to how effectively you help people achieve and excel. If leadership is about something bigger than you, coaching is a path to demonstrate your commitment to it. You do what needs to be done to make sure the other person comes away wiser and more self-aware. Sometimes, that means being patient and allowing them to grow at their own pace. Other times, it means stepping in to bring change proactively.

Great coaches take risks. They build on what exists. They are learners themselves. That's what defines a coaching culture: the default position of everyone in the organization is to listen, share experiences, suggest paths of exploration, and enthusiastically participate in each other's self-discovery and growth. As a leader, it's your job to model that.

Coaching Culture in WFH

When your team is scattered to the four winds, doing their own thing in their own environment, they are inherently more autonomous. Especially when they're getting used to working on their own, away from the support system and safety net of their coworkers, the last thing you want to do is increase their sense of dependency on their leaders. Success in WFH demands a tribe of self-starters who can sustain motivation and the drive for excellence and get results independently. Solving their problems for them is not only demotivating but in some ways insulting. You're forcing your approach to problem-solving on people whose intrinsic worth and confidence is based on becoming more independent.

Empowering people to succeed when they're largely under their own supervision means playing to their strengths. While coaching used to be about the coach, in WFH especially, it's very much about the *coached*. In the WFH world, a leader in a coaching culture is:

- A willing, generous-spirited guide, listener, and questioner who assists others in discovering their own exceptional ability and capacity.
- Proactive and rich in experience sharing and useful takeaways.
- A source of great content, storytelling, and lessons. You are not present to reinforce thinking after the coaching time is done, so any information or teaching you provide needs to be incredibly impactful.
- The one who takes heat for mistakes while giving the credit for wins to the team.

In a distributed organization, this service-first ethos is like operational software that helps everyone be optimally effective and achieve the same goals they would if they were working side by side. Listening, teaching, and allowing people to find their way also creates a background noise of respect within the organization. Everyone knows that the intention of the org is to help them grow, learn, and be their best, even in a WFH environment, because management trusts them to handle their business. Self-reliance is in the air people breathe.

Finally, coaching culture reveals *coachability*. Not everyone can be coached. It's the coach's job to win, not to raise kids, and you can't coach the uncoachable. If people can be coached, they will be. If they can't, they don't belong on the team. A coaching mindset and culture are a great way to sort out who fits and who doesn't.

Maintaining Boundaries
and Reaching over Them

There's a good reason coaching culture and mindset is the second Pillar: the most important person you will coach in self-reflection is yourself. Growing into leadership requires seeing, knowing, and respecting your limits. When great leaders can follow another leader who knows and demonstrates a better way, they do. They acknowledge it, embrace it, and practice gratitude.

So much of coaching is about just being present, listening, and asking the right questions. You're a sounding board, the audience for the play, and a storyteller, not a drill sergeant. That's tough for many executives because they're used to having all eyes on them when they enter a room. Instead, your job is to coach yourself to be a better coach and get people comfortable enough to say, "I don't know, what do you think?"

It took a while for me to reach that point, and I sort of got there (it's a work in progress) thanks in part to a coaching program developed by Cassandra Wit when she was JumpCrew's director of operations. It was our first effort at developing a coaching mindset for all new managers. The program, which included some videos and role play exercises, helped me maintain better boundaries—for instance, when I had skip-level meetings with non-direct reports around the organization, something we encourage our leaders to do. Basically, I honed my ability to ask the kind of probing questions that allow someone to consider different outcomes from different courses of action as opposed to suggesting actions.

Now, instead of asking a question and suggesting the answer, I'm more like a reporter asking follow-up questions, digging deeper into people's concerns, motivations, and prior experiences. Just being present, listening, and letting things move organically but always communicating, even if it's not always verbal communication. That level of patience and perception were missing from my "fail fast, win faster" mindset.

So much of coaching is about just being present, letting things flow, and resisting the natural boss tendency to be in control. Remember, you're surrendering control. That's one reason online gatherings at JumpCrew became warmer, friendlier, and more enjoyable. "There's a difference when you see someone every day and they can ask you a question in the hallway," Cassie says. "You can provide more answers. You can show up as an authentic leader. You can have that, 'David, how you doing?' moment and share experiences, which is a way of coaching.

"Now, reverse that if you don't see someone every day," she continues,

> Now it might be one-on-one coaching, asking about their work life balance. What are they doing outside of work? What do you like when you close your computer every day? Go to the gym? Meet friends for coffee? How are you still creating connections outside of the office? Instead of just making it about having this temporary virtual workspace with employees in California and Virginia and Florida, it's more about making sure that people have the right work-life balance and that they're not working all night. My job before this was work from home, and I struggled. So I have that experiential learning that I can share with people. That's coaching, too.

In other words, coaching in the context of a coaching culture is about giving people what they need, not what you *think* they need because they're often not the same thing. How do you do that? Keep reading.

Deep Dive

THE UNCOACHABLES

No, we're not talking Kevin Costner as Elliot Ness and Robert De Niro as Capone. Uncoachables are people who just won't accept even the subtlest pushes toward their own growth, who can't hear any opinion that suggests they should change how they do things. Chris Coffey and Frank Wagner at the Stakeholder Centered Coaching certification program have identified four indicators that someone is uncoachable:

1. They don't think they have a problem. Whatever they're doing is working for them, so why would they do things differently? They're probably blind to any collateral damage, not because they're bad people but because it doesn't occur to them that they could be the cause.

2. They're already going in the wrong direction. These folks are invested in whatever bad strategy they've been following, and they're not likely to change now. It's the "sunk cost fallacy" in action.

3. They're a bad fit for the gig. If someone is sticking with a job they don't like or aren't good at, it doesn't matter why. Their presence will harm morale and productivity. They don't belong in your org, and no amount of coaching will change that. Do yourself and them a favor and show them the door.

4. They blame everybody else. I think this is the worst of the uncoachables. Nothing is ever their fault, so you'll never get them to see the error of their ways. Send them packing.[2]

I'd like to add one more to the list:

5. Blind arrogance. Sometimes, you'll run across someone who thinks he's smarter and more capable than you (or might think acting that way is what's required) even when all the evidence suggests otherwise. All your coaching and insights are dismissed or met with scorn. So you kill this person and hide the body in—I'm kidding! If you can uncover the reason for the arrogance, there's hope, but that's not your job. Therapy is not coaching. Experience suggests that the years of programming that resulted in the arrogance you and your team are experiencing won't be solved with a little coaching. So, if you value the other members of the team, say goodbye to this person.

Coaching Is Just Good Business

A coaching culture is based on the idea that leaders are there to serve the employees' ability to grow, become more autonomous, and reach peak capability. In the end, the more capable and engaged the workforce is, the more its leaders can grow, better the company's profit, market share, customer satisfaction, product quality, or whatever metric you choose. A coaching culture is an ecosystem that allows the organization to be effective, cohesive, and accelerate achievement.

That's why it's surprising that so few companies lean into coaching as one of the ways they engage with their people. In an i4cp report, *Creating a Coaching Culture*,[3] only 20 percent of the 274 respondents rated their companies highly on using coaching effectively, with 37 percent stating they were barely effective or not effective at all. These results are mirrored in how well companies model a coaching culture, with just 23 percent in the highest ranks and 42 percent hanging onto the bottom rung.

For companies without an existing coaching culture, embracing it could require a wholesale transformation of how their leaders approach their organizations and their people. Changing a culture is much harder than building one from scratch. A coaching culture requires embedding reflective leadership in the DNA of most of your leaders. It also means you must be eager to hire people more capable than you and to enable those you're coaching to become better and more effective than you are. As a leader, you become great by building teams of people who can challenge you, outthink you, blow past you. Great CEOs don't hire less capable or deferential people any more than great basketball coaches recruit guys who can't shoot. Great leaders look to hire challengers, learners—smart, hungry, driven learners who might one day replace them.

This stuff *works*. Weaving a fabric of coaching into the everyday interactions of an office—or a virtual office—is like pouring high-octane fuel booster into a car's gas tank. A study by the Human Capital Institute and the International Coach Federation[4] found that organizations with strong coaching cultures report revenue growth well above their industry peer group and significantly higher employee engagement—62 percent of employees reporting high levels of engagement versus only half with the non-coaching companies.

If people are any organization's chief resource, then a coaching culture is a secret weapon for not only developing those people but finding them in the first place. Coaching-capable leaders get that in any organization, employees' actions are always about themselves first. That's just the reality. Even in a company like Google or Apple with an engaged workforce and a strong sense of mission, most people look out for themselves first. Of course they do! If coding an incredible app or designing a next-level electric car helps the company make millions, that's great, but every employee's first interest is naturally, laudably, their own *self*-interest.

That means your role is to help them meet their most cherished goals. Do that, and you'll swim in satisfaction, achievement, and professional success. Build a reputation as a leader with whom new hires can thrive, be themselves, learn and pursue excellence and . . . man, you'll have opened doors to growth you didn't even know existed.

Coaching and Managing are not the Same

Coaching prioritizes the sharing of experiential feedback ahead of giving top-down direction and advice giving. Instead of telling someone how you would address situation they're dealing with, you might share a story about how you dealt with a similar headache and let your listeners draw their own conclusions. You're not problem-solving in order to demonstrate your competence or to diminish anyone.

That's why coaching and managing are not the same thing. Managing is transactional. We manage to behavioral outcomes. If I want a subordinate to act in a certain way, I simply incentivize the action I want and put up disincentives for the action I don't want. If he does what I want, he gets a reward. *Transactional.* Subordinates are not required think analytically, develop strategy, or challenged to even understand strategy.

On the other hand, at JumpCrew we aspire to coach for *personal transformation.* Coaching someone isn't so much about what the person does as it's about who they are becoming. In a way, you're trying to make yourself obsolete—to nurture, teach, and encourage a tribe of workers so insightful, brave, and inspired that they don't need you to lead them. They can lead themselves. When this is working, you get to cheerlead and practice gratitude . . . or maybe move to a distant tropical island for a while.

Of course, there's a caveat here. Sometimes leaders don't have the luxury or the time to gently guide and coach their people. Sometimes you'll have to make an executive decision that's not consistent with what a subordinate wants—as we know, business can be very time sensitive, and personal growth isn't. But the success or failure of that call will depend on the trust, confidence, connection, and respect you have earned through a coaching mindset.

Your relationship will determine how someone digests an order that goes against what they want or your normal approach as a coach, gentle advisor, or quiet guru. If you've been clear and consistent in your intent, you'll probably win support as long as you quickly and clearly communicate why you're making an executive decision. If not, you could undermine your otherwise collaborative and beneficial relationship with what's perceived as a brute reversion to a command-control model—a betrayal. Your investment in the personal relationship is critical. That's capital available to use it when you need it.

If you want an example of the coach as wise teacher with an iron will for making people better, you would be hard-pressed to find a better one than the late UCLA coach John Wooden, who I mentioned earlier. If you have a chance, listen to Wooden's talks. Leading his teams to a 664–162 record and named NCAA College Basketball Coach of the Year six times, the legendary Wooden was famous for his outwardly gentle, positive, affirming nature. Unlike screamers like Indiana University coach Bobby Knight, he believed in guiding athletes with a firm hand and a lot of love and support. His goal was to help them become more fully realized people, not just basketball players. He demanded hard work on the court while insisting that his players do their best academically—an anomaly in a time when too many college athletes are shuttled into cupcake making majors so they could make grades and retain their eligibility.

In order to inspire his players to give their all, Wooden developed a teaching model he called the Pyramid of Success. It's a literal pyramid with qualities like *industriousness, loyalty,* and *cooperation* at the base, moving up through traits like *self-control, skill,* and *poise* to *competitive greatness* at the top. Around the edges are other traits: *reliability, patience, integrity, sincerity,* and the like. Nowhere on the pyramid does it say anything like *leaping ability, jump shot,* or *crossover dribble.* The pyramid, and Wooden's entire coaching ethos, was about character, not basketball. Build great young men, he reasoned, and you'd build great basketball players in the process.

Another wonderful example of this mentality is San Antonio Spurs head coach Greg Popovich. With a pedigree that includes learning at the feet of Larry Brown at the University of Kansas, you'd expect Pop to be a terrific coach, but that's not what makes him great. He's one of those rare coaches who considers his job to be creating other coaches. Back in 2019, I had the opportunity to attend a game where the Spurs played the Memphis Grizzlies—a short jump from Nashville and a cheap enough courtside ticket for me to buy two tickets near the end of the San Antonio bench. For two and a half hours, Rob and I were able to observe close-up one of the greatest NBA coaches of all time in action.

But what's funny is that watching Pop coach his team was the most boring part of the evening. He didn't really do anything. His assistants ran the timeouts, and when the players came to the sidelines, they were in control of the huddle. They were calm, insightful, and everyone seemed to have an equal voice. They could have been in a JumpCrew best practices meeting on Google Meet. I was floored. Pop's coaching had all been done before the game. He had taught his players to coach each other. During the action, Pop sat quietly while the players not in the game shouted out the opposition defense, called out screens, and guided the motion of the offense too.

The net output of Pop's style was astonishing. Over his twenty-four-year tenure, the Spurs made the playoffs twenty-two consecutive seasons and won five NBA titles. That speaks to the success of building a great coaching culture.

Again, this is coaching that roams far, far beyond the game, whether that game is basketball or sales. Being a coach—from the perspective of someone like Wooden or Popovich or the "Zen master" himself, former Chicago Bulls and LA Lakers coach Phil Jackson—means focusing on heart and character first. You can teach skills. You can't teach character.

At this level of coaching, the end activity, whether it's business or sports, is always the *last* thing taught. Coaching is a tool to helping human beings realize their full potential, and the top-line goals are *always* self-awareness, wisdom, and discipline. As Coach Wooden wrote, "Talent is God-given; be humble. Fame is man-given; be thankful. Conceit is self-given; be careful."[5]

Coaching Through Conflict

But while stories like that of John Wooden sound peaceful and wholesome, you know there was tension and times when people simply could not agree or would not get along. Coaching during times of conflict can seem impossibly challenging because it feels like you're called on to get your hands dirty, give orders, and solve problems so everything can return to normal.

But as with everything else in this area, the coach's first law is to stand back and try, when possible, to allow people to solve things on their own—including resolving conflict. As Daniel Griffith, an attorney and human resources expert, writes, "Managers must take responsibility for helping employees develop the capability to address their conflict situations on their own whenever possible."[6]

Some people aren't comfortable with conflict, so they try and avoid it. But it's the leader's job to deescalate conflict, to be a source of reason, calm, and communication—a referee, if I'm going to continue with the sports metaphor. Resolving conflict is part of the job, but one key is to invest in the intervention, not the outcome. You can't control the outcome. You're dealing with strong, smart, independent adults, and the only way to guarantee the outcome you want is to force your will on them, which is not a long-term solution. It shatters morale and makes people feel that they're being treated like children. Forget about the outcome and concentrate on a process that fosters clarity, communication, and understanding.

Start by establishing things you can agree on. Lead with what's positive and what's working. Acknowledge the points of view of all parties, regardless of your opinion. Remember, everyone is right in his or her own mind, and if backing down means being proved wrong, then people will dig in and refuse to compromise. Put another way, when someone says something that seems batshit crazy, remember that to them, it makes total sense. That's why resolving conflict isn't about winning but empathizing.

Finally, be careful with the words you choose. The last thing you want is to trigger more defensiveness in anyone, and certain words do that. Be careful to avoid words that imply judgment or blame, and certainly hold your temper. Calm, cool, and impartial—that's how you resolve conflict.

Elements of the Coaching Mindset

Release of ego. The outcome isn't about you or anything you can control. And the endgame of a particular business challenge isn't a referendum on how awesome you are. Focus on the person or people who stand to learn from the situation and set your own needs aside.

Perspective. A situation or problem might appear huge to a someone who's less experienced and in the middle of it, and it could overwhelm their ability to think clearly and see the big picture. Your job is to keep the issue at arm's length and not get pulled into the drama or fear, so you can see beyond the immediate to the larger picture. That's incredibly useful when you're trying to calm a stressful situation or get someone past an obstacle that's tripped them up repeatedly.

Over-communicate. What's worse than not hearing what you want to hear from a partner, coworker, boss, bank, vendor, or customer? *Hearing nothing at all.* Feeling like you're being ignored. Nature abhors a vacuum, and the human mind will tend to fill a vacuum in communication with irrational meditations on the worst-case scenario. Just ask anyone who's been on the receiving end of increasingly irate texts from a significant other because they didn't respond while they were driving in heavy traffic. The cure for you, the coach, is to communicate excessively, consistently, and using whatever means the learner finds most helpful. If they like to hear your voice, get on the phone. Avoid radio silence; it leads to fear. Instead, be clear, consistent, and propulsive—always moving the conversation forward to the next topic or to resolution.

Juror mentality. Some people have the capacity to hover between both sides of an argument without passing judgment or committing to either one. I call that the *juror mentality*. For a coach, not jumping to a conclusion allows you to take in everything as a neutral party and provide insights and guidance that are as untainted by natural human bias as possible.

Caring feedback. So much of successful coaching is about intention. What's your intention when you speak with that employee in your office or on Zoom? To impress? To be the hero? To listen, or to share? Maybe to inspire the employee to take a risk and try something new? Intention is the difference between success and failure, and that comes through in the type of feedback you give. It should always be honest but expressed in a way that lifts the learner up and makes him or her feel more capable or more hopeful. Phrases like "I know you have the talent to get this done" and "I'm confident you can crack this" go a long, long way to keeping someone inspired even when they're discouraged. Pay attention to the words you use, and offer feedback that empowers.

Growth, not wins. As with John Wooden, the road to the end goal isn't always what it seems. His end goal was to win basketball games, but he got there via a long detour through discipline, learning, and character building. Your first job is to produce people who can think for themselves, push back against negativity, remain focused and disciplined, and believe in themselves. Wins will come.

Generosity. You're already an achiever or you wouldn't be in a position to lead others. So you're already farther along in your journey than many of those you'll be coaching. Get yourself in a generous frame of mind that appreciates the value of everybody you work with, even if they are not superstars. Not everyone can be world-class, but that doesn't mean they don't have a great deal to offer the organization.

Asking and guiding, not telling and fixing. There's an old story often told in recovery meetings. A man is walking down the street and falls into a hole. He quickly climbs out and moves on. Then he falls into a deeper hole. Mad at himself, he clambers out and keeps walking down the street. Then he falls into yet another hole, this one so deep that he really has to work to escape, and he's furious at himself. But he keeps walking along the same street, and eventually tumbles into *another* hole, this one so deep that he's not sure he can get out. Angry beyond words at his clumsiness, he struggles and eventually climbs out, sweaty and filthy. Finally, he turns and walks down a different street.

> Your job is to help people turn down the other street before they get dirty, and you won't do that by telling them where to go all the time. You do that by changing how they look at things.

Gratitude. You're blessed to have people willing to listen and to have experience and perspective to share. Don't lose sight of that. Practicing gratitude and providing recognition are a huge part of a leader's responsibility.

Patience. You're there to empower self-discovery, to open the door. The other person has to walk through. They will do that in their own good time. Be patient.

Campbell Soup Does It Right

A corporate culture dedicated to coaching and to the mentality that makes coaching possible is a breeding ground for excellence. One of the best examples of this is Campbell Soup Company, which has been a staple of American households since the 1880s. When in the 1990s the company's fortunes sagged, shortsighted leaders did what they do: they focused on short-term goals. They lowered quality standards, stopped pushing for product innovation, and reduced advertising budgets. That stopped the bleeding, but wasn't sustainable. Plus, as all that happened, employees became more and more disengaged. Something had to change.

Change began when Campbell's brought in Doug Conant to be CEO. Conant centered the company's turnaround on the creation of a corporate culture focused on character, competence, and teamwork. Leaders were expected to inspire trust, create direction, drive organizational alignment, build organization vitality, execute with excellence, and produce extraordinary results. But the most important piece may have been the Campbell Promise. As Conant said in an interview, "It's about Campbell valuing people and people valuing Campbell. As a company, we need to tangibly demonstrate to our employees that we value their agenda before we can ever expect them to value our agenda."

Campbell's also launched its CEO Institute, a coaching and training model based around the notion that how someone leads is based on who they are. No one thrives by being shoehorned into a program created by someone else. "We're each a creation of our environment—how we were raised, our wiring, our DNA—and the model that works for me is not going to be exactly the model for you," Conant says. "You've got to achieve a level of authenticity where you're at one with your leadership model. The CEO Institute is about helping our people create their own leadership models. Our hope is that they'll create a model that will be in harmony with the Campbell model."[7]

That last statement says so much. Conant hopes the leaders he trains will be in harmony with the company. That's right. You can't tell people how to grow or what path will be right for them. The best you can do is give them what you have to give and hope they land in a place that works for your organization. The rest is up to them.

Campbell Soup Company embodies so many of the qualities that define a strong, reflective coaching culture:

It's opportunistic. The Hudson Institute[8] teaches a concept called "spot coaching," in which coaching is offered in the moment on a just-in-time basis, in sync with the real needs of the person receiving the coaching. Coaching cultures leverage every opportunity to pass on ideas, share stories, or inspire—meetings, random encounters in the halls, or, in a WFH environment, the ten minutes before a Zoom meeting officially begins when everyone's talking about how they spent their weekend.

It's permission based. As I've said, asking someone for their permission to share your view or before you give advice is a powerful act of respect and esteem. "Would you mind if I gave you some feedback?" is a typical question. In sales speak, if the person says "Yes, please," then you have an upfront verbal contract that opens the door for someone to accept a different opinion. If the person declines, then by walking away you're still showing that you respect their autonomy. It's a win-win.

It includes modeling. Modeling means demonstrating by your own example in an optimized, elevated way so they can recognize a better version of their own thinking. If the principles of coaching prohibit you from telling someone directly that they are doing something unwise or behaving a way that harms team chemistry, modeling is another way to teach. For example, if an employee is stressed out about a task and acting abruptly and impatiently, modeling would mean that you approach that same task with calm and good humor. You're modeling more productive behavior, showing the employee that there's another way to tackle this challenge.

It features reward for character, not just performance. Jump-Crew is a sales organization, so we have to produce and meet our KPIs. That said, if that's all we reward, we're building a community that's completely transactional. That tells people that if they don't meet their KPIs, they have little worth. So we go beyond performance to reward our people for being good people—for growth, insight, compassion. Campbell's and other companies like Patagonia reward their people for values that align with the company's values, which sends a different message: *We're in this together, and you matter.*

It's aligned and honest. Finally, great coaching cultures arise in organizations that walk their talk, that express a set of corporate values and then live up to them every day. Employees will quickly check out of an organization that they see as hypocritical, but if you're backing up values and mission statements with action, you'll win the respect of your people, and they'll be more likely to listen to you.

And remember, great coaches are also learners. You don't find the sage at the bottom of the mountain. The great teachers make the hard climb themselves before they ask anyone to listen to them. Now, let's switch gears and look at how coaching culture plays out in WFH.

Chapter Six

COACHING A REMOTE ORGANIZATION

So how does coaching work in a WFH environment? I think the best way to kick off the discussion is to share a real story about a key JumpCrew player, Rob Solberg.

Rob, like me and like most of his JumpCrew peers, started his journey as a sales guy. He had managed before, but when he approached JumpCrew, a management position wasn't available. But Rob was willing to earn his stripes in sales and smart enough to know that once he had, his street cred would be an asset in leading a team. Fast forward three years and Rob looked like a star. He was a key part of the leadership team, overseeing critical sales and marketing teams for Fortune 500 companies, solid gold social media brands, and high-flyer tech firms.

Rob is an endearing, caring guy with an inhuman capacity to out-work everyone else—an authentic high-energy, fast-talking leader with a great sense of humor. A self-described showman, he worked the room better than anyone I had ever seen, and his humor and energy were great additions to our in-person all-hands meetings. However, the high-voltage persona on which his success depended would be seriously challenged by two life-changing situations.

The first was a potentially serious health problem Rob had struggled with for years. When it flared up, he was forced to slow down, and the condition lingered for years. I had a doctor friend connect him with a medical team that cured many of the symptoms he was experiencing. Rob came to New York for the procedure, and we talked in-depth for the first time over a celebratory dinner. I realized that my all-drive, all-the-time approach to business may have caused the stress that had contributed to his last flareup. While he was onboarding and scaling our most important client, I had grilled him about things he couldn't yet focus on like KPI metrics, lifetime customer value, feedback loops, and our ability to scale the business. Now my focus was his health and aligning his well-being with JumpCrew's goals.

Rob had become one of the executives I met with on my monthly trips to our Nashville HQ, and when COVID ended that routine, we seamlessly transitioned our coaching sessions to thirty-minute video chats twice a month. However, Rob's ability to translate his style of leadership to the new WFH reality was more problematic. His natural leadership style feeds off his charisma, positive energy, and his great sense of humor; he's at his best in a crowded, busy room filled with salespeople, all getting a charge from each other's adrenaline. Being forced to lead his team of relatively inexperienced managers from home went against his natural need to have a tactile, physical presence in the room. In the fall of 2020, he acknowledged to me that he had been humbled by the need to change how he led his people.

Now, I think it's a truism to say that successful sales reps have vast reservoirs of self-confidence. You don't get to the top of the profession unless you're close to brimming over with the stuff, unless you can step into any room, no matter how unusual the circumstances, and convince everyone that your insight, support, and dependability are critical to the spinning of their globe. In my experience, that near-arrogance often stems from a bit of insecurity or lack of self-awareness. However, when someone like Rob does discover a well of vulnerability and self-awareness, it's a beautiful, transformative moment. This is a how our session unfolded:

ME: *How you doing, Rob?*

ROB: *Sometimes these meetings are so polarizing. There is always truth in what you say, and I leave feeling great and bad about myself.*

ME: *I hear you.*

ROB: *I am not as analytical as Adolfo, yet I am not missing the point. I am struggling because I am lean with support and short on managers.*

ME: *Maybe this is our time. You have never joined a Circle or come to any of our leadership trainings or workshops. Last month* you cancelled our session to fit in another sales meeting and never rescheduled. Yesterday at the end of our session, you asked if we could talk again today. Maybe that's a sign; let's go deeper. How do you make demands?

ROB: *Going from fixing accounts issues to jumping on a pitch is emotionally taxing, and I am doing my best. I am doing exactly what Rob wants me to do: lower churn and increase cash flow.*

ME: *Yes. Are you doing it most effectively? What kind of stuff do you do to invest in yourself?*

ROB: *I can't find twenty minutes. I haven't read a book in four years. I'm either actively working or recovering. [Without being in the office.] I am unable to delineate between what's good and bad for me to schedule. My style is bopping around the office giving high-fives. It's being available and visible. This style is taxing. It's a completely different muscle group. It's always been showmanship, and in an in-person environment, that works beautifully. That doesn't work anymore. I need to reinvent myself. My first seven months of this was a period of self-awareness.*

I have taken inventory of what's working and what's not working. There's still a lot of discovery to do, but I realized it all needs to be revisited. What's next is there has to be a commitment. I have to commit to what's needed to be changed. I need to leave myself conscious space to work through change. The rational part of me says to block time. The part of me that knows me says I should just plow through, but then I am exhausted.

ME: *Rob, why doesn't LeBron play the whole game?*

ROB: *I know why.*

ME: *How do you think he feels when he goes out in the second quarter and they are up by ten, but when he comes back, they are tied?*

ROB: *I've done harder things than this in the past, and I am stumped.*

ME: *This is the big battle. It's about being clear, holding people accountable and prioritizing yourself.*

ROB: *Could we talk again Monday morning?*

What you don't see in this conversation is all the previous work Rob and I did in past sessions. But this call was where it came to fruition. He realized that leading from home required him to change how he thought, how he acted, and how he saw himself. He had learned that he needed to schedule breaks between meetings and slow down so other people could set the pace, and he was going all in to make the change. I was happy to coach him through it, and it felt great that he trusted me to help him in the transition.

You're the Vessel, Not the Water

What may also stand out about that exchange is that during the most pivotal part of that session, where Rob bravely articulated his struggles and his commitment to change, I said nothing. That's both the toughest part and the most rewarding part about a coaching culture: You're not there to fix things.

Coaching culture came early at JumpCrew, long before COVID-19, because we realized that, while we had a strong pool of folks who were powerful problem solvers, there's an inherent conflict between problem-solving and growing the org. There's a limit to what a problem solver can do as a manager and as a leader. When you're the only source of problem-solving, you limit your organization's capacity to accelerate growth. It's like asking Michael Jordan to take every shot.

My drive around creating sense of urgency (and to a lesser degree, being a perfectionist) led me to become the chief problem solver for much of my career. But while that may have satisfied my ego and felt like the quick fix, it bred negative emotions among my peers because the experience didn't leave them feeling good, smart, or empowered. I worked this way with a good deal of success—in small companies—but looking back, I believe it limited my success and cost me some bigger wins too.

People, top to bottom, become inspired in an environment that supports their ability to become better. That's precisely what you should encourage because as your team becomes more skilled, capable, and better at leading, they'll become the source of the innovations and ideas that will take your organization to the next level. But when you problem solve, you reduce those opportunities, lose the best of them, and demotivate the rest. Coaching culture is critical to a remote organization because it empowers individual contributors to stretch, risk, and find their next gear. When you coach, you send an implied but crystal-clear message: "I trust you to figure this out and do it your way."

That's why I managed that exchange with Rob the way I did. A few years back, I might not have had the patience to lay back and let him talk himself through his epiphany. I might have tried to tell him how to think. But I'm (a little) wiser and (a little) more self-aware now. By saying nothing but being an affirming presence, I created a safe space where Rob solved the puzzle and reached a terrific conclusion—that he needed to do more work—on his own. That conclusion was a thousand times more meaningful because he came to it on his own. That's the job of the leader-as-coach: to be a vessel of self-discovery. Help people ask the right questions, support them with your presence, then shut your mouth, hang back, and let them grow.

It's like being the head coach of a winning team: you're not the focus/star because you're not the one on the field, nor should you be. But it's the way to win. You're the model for learning and investing in everyone else's growth and success. That's the definition of leadership.

The BLM Email and Opportunistic Coaching

Just like everything else, that general coaching ethos has to evolve somewhat in a WFH environment. The basic principle of coaching remains the same—you're there to share and guide, not to solve problems—but when people are based remotely, leaders need to be more planned and deliberate in reaching out to share. You can't just walk up and lean on somebody's cubicle wall when they're blocked and drop a pearl of wisdom to help them have that "Aha!" moment. Coaching has become part of the underlying fabric of your culture, because without that "leadership has my back and is there to guide me" feeling, people who are already physically isolated can feel mentally and spiritually isolated too.

In WFH, smart leaders treat every instance of communication and interaction as a coaching opportunity:

- Meetings
- Companywide emails
- Slack discussions
- Team strategy calls
- One-on-one calls

One of the best examples of this in my recent memory came from Rob Henderson in the form of an email to all of JumpCrew. A few days earlier, George Floyd had been killed and massive Black Lives Matter protests had filled the streets. People at JumpCrew were on edge, and someone needed to put the anxiety out in the open. This is what Rob wrote:

As I'm guessing many of us have, I've spent a lot of time trying to make sense of this horrible situation in which we find ourselves as a nation—and genuinely asking myself where do we go from here? Simply saying nice things like "this is terrible" and "we need to do better" will not fix the problem.

We really do need to do better.

I woke up this morning feeling a sense of responsibility to in fact do better.

Sitting and hoping that the world will change will not help; as individuals, we each possess the ability and power to change the world around us. We must take accountability to be positive forces during these challenging times. We must reject hate, racism and oppression in our society.

There are things each of us can do:

- *Be kinder*
- *Show more empathy*
- *Educate ourselves*
- *Provide opportunities to those who would otherwise not be afforded them*
- *Most importantly VOTE for government representatives that align with your values*

While sometimes we lose our way as individuals, groups, families or even as a nation, I choose to believe that there is goodness in every single one of us. Let's each take personal accountability for the world around us and fight to be positive forces for good.

Change starts today and change starts with us.
Please contact me directly if you would like to discuss.

Thanks,
Rob Henderson, CEO

That's extraordinary. It's what I call *coaching in the moment*. It's taking advantage of something happening in real time and turning it into an opportunity to model reflective behavior, share, or offer your own insight. BLM has nothing to do directly with JumpCrew, but of course what was happening was on everyone's mind, and certainly not just our Black employees, because we're all human beings and we care about each other. Diversity was an original JumpCrew value. If someone hadn't said something, a cloud might have hung over the company for weeks as people wondered if our silence on the issue signaled our ambivalence.

By stepping up, Rob was coaching in the moment. He was

modeling self-awareness and introspection for everyone else in the community. Not a word of "you should do this, too" needed to be said. Opportunistic coaching takes unexpected events and turns them into subtle, covert coaching opportunities by relying on the key values of coaching culture: humility, self-reflection, sharing, and doing your own work. This thinking can transform many common, even negative, occurrences in the daily life of a business into windows to impart quiet, heartfelt, insights:

- Customer complaints
- Layoffs
- Traumatic outside events
- Failing to win a new client
- Changes like a relocation

You have to pick your spots and choose your words carefully, as Rob did. Note that most of what he said in that email was about how *he* was feeling and what he thought *his* responsibilities were. That's black belt coaching.

The Mr. Miyagi Effect and "Owning Your Shit"

Speaking of black belts, maybe you remember *The Karate Kid*. Not the remake with Jaden Smith, but the 1984 original with the wonderful Pat Morita as Mr. Miyagi. If you're familiar with it, you probably remember the infamous "wax on, wax off" scenes. Mr. Miyagi, the unassuming Japanese man who becomes a *sensei* ("teacher") to the hero, Daniel, begins the young man's karate training by having him engage in a series of menial tasks that appear to have nothing to do with learning the martial arts: waxing Mr. Miyagi's collection of vintage cars, painting his fence, sanding his wooden floor. Every movement is deliberate and intentional, but a resentful Daniel just thinks he's been turned into an unpaid servant.

Of course, what the young man fails to see is that he's not only learning basic karate blocking techniques and building up important muscles, but also developing both physical and mental endurance. When Miyagi finally reveals the martial arts techniques concealed in the repetitive movements, Daniel is astonished. He had no idea he was learning karate.

In a coaching culture, the Mr. Miyagi Effect refers to the phenomenon that true learning and growth rarely occur due to some lesson or "do this" piece of wisdom that you impart directly. Remember, that's not the coach's job. Advice and feedback not rooted in first-hand experience comes across as heavy-handed and insincere, especially when it's not explicitly asked for, like a parent lecturing a truculent teen. In fact, studies suggest that when advice is given and not taken, relationships suffer, and that fewer people in groups are willing to share their opinion when advice is given to any one person.[1] That's why my previous suggestion about asking permission applies universally.

There's a time and a place to coach *overtly*, usually when someone is expecting it. Those are scheduled calls or the kind of individual work I did with Rob. *Covert* coaching, on the other hand, can happen at any time, usually via the leader sharing a personal experience—a self-deprecating story about a blunder that became a lesson. In those cases, you're simply coaching by example, being the change. Indirect learning occurs when you as the leader are demonstrating how to reflect, question, be vulnerable, and be open to change simply by who you are and how you behave.

This kind of self-aware behavior has another name, courtesy of Dr. Brad Reedy: "owning your shit." Because he is a trained therapist and an intensely mindful man, Brad is the first person to own his issues, his trauma, and his difficulty breaking past patterns—his "shit." We all have shit we're charged with handling, he says, and the first responsibility of any leader who aspires to be an effective coach is to "own" the work he or she needs to do: to be conscious of it, address it, publicly admit it, not retreat from it when said shit triggers a negative response to a situation, and accept feedback openly and even gratefully.

"I will never get rid of my shit," he says. "I'm just much more conscious of it. My team is conscious of my shit because we've talked about it. They know when I'm doing my shit and vice versa. My business partner will say to me one every once in a while, 'Brad, you don't have to do that,' and it's really healing when he says that. What I'm usually doing is trying to prove myself."

One of the qualities I really admire about Brad is his self-honesty. He doesn't shy away from his weaknesses or blind spots. That's crucial for great leaders and great coaches. "If you can talk about your shit, you can solve anything," he says. "You get past it. One of the greatest minds to ever walk to earth is the Dalai Lama. If you listen to him talk, he will make fifteen to twenty jokes about his idiocy throughout the course of the time. If he trips, he will point it out and laugh at it. I once saw him at a live event, and he talked about how old and decrepit he's getting. You have to lean into what's horrible about you. Put that stuff on the table and talk about what it's like. Because it will come up. When it does, you're cool."

What would leadership look like if the mark of the leader was not being the smartest or the most powerful person in the room? Maybe instead, great leading is about being the first one to step to the mic and say, "This is how I'm messed up and why, this is what it will look like when I'm scared, and I own that." What if self-awareness and radical honesty became the defining characteristics of leading, remote organization or not? I think it would change everything.

Good Intentions Breed Beneficial Actions

Jerry Colonna is a Renaissance man. Apart from being the author of a great book about coaching and one of the founders of a corporate coaching company, both of which are called Reboot, he was a cofounder of one of the most successful venture capital firms in NY, partnering with Fred Wilson to start Flatiron Partners before joining the private equity arm of JP Morgan Chase. He has spent two decades working to help entrepreneurs and executives lead with courage and humanity.

Jerry crafted Reboot's coaching formula, which combines practical skills, radical self-inquiry, and shared experiences to help people enhance their leadership ability and develop greater resilience— all ideas central to my own ideas about coaching. So he knows a thing or two about what coaching really is. He's also an exceptional speaker and all-around brilliant guy, so I knew I had to interview him for this book. When I did, he dropped this wisdom on me: "What I often teach my clients is that a leader's job ultimately is to create the conditions for great people to do the best work of their lives," he says. "What we've just done is altered the definition of success from financial return to human development. The organization becomes a field of play for people to grow. I happen to believe, and evidence shows, that you can get very good returns on investment by creating the organization as a field of play for the best people to do the best work of their lives. Because the counter argument is equally true. We create environments that are toxic, good people who have a choice to work elsewhere will. And I don't know how you create the best organization when your best people are constantly leaving.

"A good coach would ask a client, 'Would you rather people leave or stay out of love or leave or stay out of fear?'" Jerry continues. "When we were in economic times where people did not have choices, we might have stayed in a toxic environment out of fear. That is a perfectly reasonable, rational leadership strategy—less evolved, but traditional. It evolved from a misunderstanding of strong leadership.

"A lot of people look to the military and say, 'Command and control,' but they don't understand the military," he goes on. "They don't understand that in the military, love is the dominant emotion—love of country, patriotism, duty, and responsibility. You don't join the military because you're afraid. And you excel in a military command and control structure because you're able to inspire. When you inculcate a coaching mentality within your leadership culture, you are creating the expectation that the leader's job is to create conditions for people to excel."

There's another word for what Jerry's talking about: *trust*. All coaching depends on a trusting relationship between the coach and the person receiving the coaching. The recipient has to trust that you're a safe receptacle for their fears and doubts, that they can be candid without negative blowback, that you will guide them without taking away their agency, and that you will keep everything confidential.

In a coaching culture, trust stands or falls on the *intent* of the coach. Jerry's thoughts on the military reflect this perfectly. Even if your Marine Corps drill instructor pushes you past your limits, you stick with it because you know his intent is not to torture you or make you cry but to help you find strength you didn't know you had—to help you be your best and be victorious on the battlefield, if it comes to that. Great coaches in a business context come to the table with one endgame in mind: helping the person they're coaching ultimately surpass them. It might not happen, but that has to be your intent. That's the only way you'll bring your A game every time. That's the reason the people you're coaching will trust you even when you're asking them to be uncomfortable, confront fears, or work harder than they have in their lives. Intent matters. Your people will pick up on it.

A great general example of this comes from Steven Berglas, PhD, a clinical psychologist and coach. In the *Harvard Business Review*, he takes to task executive coaches whose intention is to seem like they're going deep with their powerful clients while actually keeping things undemanding and superficial:

> To achieve fast results, many popular executive coaches model their interventions after those used by sports coaches, employing techniques that reject out of hand any introspective process that can take time and cause "paralysis by analysis." The idea that an executive coach can help employees improve performance quickly is a great selling point to CEOs, who put the bottom line first. Yet that approach tends to gloss over any unconscious conflict the employee might have. This can have disastrous consequences for the company in the long term and can exacerbate the psychological damage to the person targeted for help.[2]

The greatest opportunity for personal growth occurs during the time you spend reflecting on your actions and intentions when it seems like you have nothing else to talk about. For a good coach—and especially for the professional therapist—it's the periods that lack the urgency of a crisis or a deadline that create time and space for breakthroughs that are impossible when you are operating in a state of stress and anxiety.

We can see the opposite end of the spectrum in the ESPN docu-series *The Last Dance,* about Michael Jordan's final season with the Chicago Bulls. In that series, Jordan comes across as a monomaniacal jerk who is constantly challenging and pushing his teammates to the point of emotional and borderline physical abuse. Why did Scottie Pippen and the rest of the fellas put up with Michael? Because they knew his intent was to bring out their best and make them champions.

Even as he was pushing them, Jordan had his arms around his guys. He really loved them. If you come into a coaching relationship with the obvious intent to do absolute good for the person you're coaching, and you truly care about them, then you can push them very hard. There are limits, of course, but good coaches and professionally trained therapists rarely cross that line.

In a WFH environment, coaching relies even more on trust than traditional in-person coaching does. Does that seem odd? After all, the person you're coaching isn't easily accessible to you. Why is the need for trust greater? Because in a WFH world, coaching seems more transactional. Getting together on Zoom doesn't feel as organic as sitting down in a room and chatting. As the coach, it's your responsibility to compensate for the distance that WFH creates by going all in to build trust.

In doing this across the companies I am engaged with, including JumpCrew, I like to fall back on Don Miguel Ruiz's Four Agreements:

- Be impeccable with your word.
- Don't take anything personally.
- Don't make assumptions.
- Always do your best.

I have found that no matter how much of your own work you still need to do, no matter how much of an imposter you might feel like when you step to the plate on either end of a coaching session, if you do what you say you'll do, let things roll off your back, avoid assumptions, and give 110 percent, people know it. Your intent will be transparent, your actions pure, and you'll win their trust.

How You Know If Coaching Is Working

The theoretical is important, but so is the practical. After all, unless you're a trained therapist or consulting executive coach, you're not coaching your people solely for their benefit, but for you and your company's benefit. The object of a coaching culture is to create an atmosphere of collaboration and safety and to challenge your people to become better versions of themselves, problem solve, be more effective at work, and lead others to excel. A coaching culture contributes to corporate growth and personal achievement.

That's why, especially in a WFH world, you need to rely on data to tell you if coaching is as effective as you hope. It's vital to track metrics for the people and groups engaged in coaching and peer learning and watch for improvement from the outset of coaching onward. I'm not talking about watching your sales dashboard. That impact comes once you've elevated individual contributors who've benefitted from your culture, promoted reflective leaders, and benefitted from your most talented employees growing with the organization. Instead, focus on core competencies that drive success in your org and surveys about Circles and qualitative behavioral outcomes and less on short-term quantitative data. Simply put, are the people on your team doing what they say they are going to and doing it well? But even if you're in an industry where outcomes are less black and white, you can gather data.

What are your teams saying about your org? How are they rating their experience? Are they staying with your organization longer? If you're coaching leaders, is their department more productive, or is turnover down? Those are all terrific indicators that coaching is having the desired effect.

Once you have an established relationship with the person you're coaching, one that crosses the professional/personal boundary and allows you to understand the person's goals, nuances, skills, strengths, and weaknesses, start looking for the data points that will tell you if coaching is working for them. There is no hard and fast level of improvement because that will vary based on each individual's challenges, abilities and goals. However, look for:

- Higher productivity;
- Greater engagement;
- Stronger peer relationships; and
- Improved quality of work.

WFH Coaching Skills

Remember that in the end, no one expects you to have all the answers. You're the sage, not the problem solver. I can empathize with someone, but I don't have solutions for someone who's got three roommates and has to work out of her bedroom. Coaching skills are soft skills in the sense that they're fluid and personal, different for everyone. But they are also hard skills in the sense that they have a powerful impact on motivation, morale, and behavior.

There are also some practical skills that any leader-coach will require, especially in a work-from-home scenario:

Accountability and respecting agency. Every coach needs to know when and how to step back and let the person receiving the coaching know that the line is *here*. This is the point where you expect them to step up and take responsibility for their progress. This is about feel—not letting empathy debilitate someone, making your expectations clear, while also making it apparent that you'll still be available for a check-in.

> "I won't say the leader's job is to *make sure* that people excel. I don't take away individual agency," says Jerry Colonna. "The individual still has the responsibility to grow. I am a coach because of who I am, but who I am has changed because I am a coach. How I approach my former wife, how I approach my children, how I approach my partner, and how I approach my job as a CEO is all different because of how I am as a coach."

Disciplined repetition. Effective coaching is like working out to build muscle: To get results, you have to show up regularly and keep at it. Schedule regular coaching sessions, and insist that other leaders in your organization do the same. Be consistent and persistent in your discussions and the insights you share, and don't expect even the most obvious revelations to become apparent or take hold immediately. I know from personal experience that growth takes time, even if the need for it is staring you right in the face.

Mastery of multiple media. Be adept at using videoconferencing, instant messaging, group coaching software like Circl.es, and any other tools you might use.

Sharing data. If you have empirical data that shows how the people you're coaching are progressing, share it with them. At JumpCrew, our sales dashboard data is transparent and available to everyone. Think of it as weighing yourself when you're trying to lose weight, or checking the balance of your 401(k). If people know where they stand, they can set more specific goals and track their progress.

Vocal and facial neutrality. This is a big one when you're coaching remotely. It's important to manage your presence. It's already limited by remote status, so the tone of your voice and (if you're on Zoom) your facial expressions and tone are critical. You can't let hints of impatience or judgment seep into your interactions, or you'll risk altering the course of the sessions. This is another aspect of the "jury mentality" I mentioned earlier. Take in information; do not draw conclusions.

Emotional intelligence about the kind of push needed. You'll need to hone your intuition about what your learner needs in the moment. Someone to just listen? A light course correction? A pat on the back? Candid feedback? Great coaches have sensitive antennae for this. Transformation happens more often via micro-adjustments than it does via giant leaps. How do you acknowledge progress and encourage a greater commitment to growth?

"Sticky" content. You won't always be available, especially in WFH. So give each learner material they can refer to when you're not around. At JumpCrew, we emphasize Individual Learning Plans (ILPs). If you don't have the resources to develop and manage ILPs, you can always share PDF downloads, books to read, podcasts, or transcript notes of your sessions.

Listen. Speak half as much as you listen.

Finally, offer *constructive* experiential feedback. Feedback is crucial, but feedback is only constructive when people feel supported and safe. Without safety, feedback can be perceived as criticism or a threat. Seed the soil for feedback with mirroring language:

- "What I loved . . ."
- "What I learned . . ."
- "What I lost . . ."
- "Now what . . .?"

Encourage deeper exploration by sharing your own relevant experiences.

Our goal as a coach is to hear and feel what someone is saying, not to render judgment or even have an opinion. Ask permission before you offer feedback. If you don't get it, bite your tongue. Feedback that someone isn't ready to hear is pointless, and potentially detrimental.

Deep Dive
COACHING THROUGH CONFLICT

Leaders often struggle at resolving conflict because all too often they don't resolve it; they suppress it. This tends to happen when they see conflict as a verdict against their leadership when it's nothing of the kind. Conflict, in the right hands, is an opportunity to bring people together—for growth, for learning, for harmony. It starts with recognizing that what people say when they are triggered isn't about you. It's about them. So there is no reason to take their words personally. Just accept that while the other person's outburst may not make sense to you, it makes sense to them.

As an aware leader, you should be willing to acknowledge conflict but not always resolve it. Sometimes, your job is to channel it in a positive way. This is what Peter Senge refers to as "creative tension" in *The Fifth Discipline*.[3] He writes that the gap between the current reality and your vision should be a tremendous source of creative energy if both leader and followers move toward resolving that tension.

In Senge's model, imagine a rubber band stretched between your vision and your current reality. When stretched, that rubber band creates tension between what is and what could be. What does tension seek? Resolution or release. There are only two ways for the tension to be released: pull your reality toward your vision, or pull your vision toward your reality. Either way, you move. The only thing tension can't do is be still.

In any organization, conflict is rarely about the obvious but about something systemic as part of a process that creates friction or something personal and unresolved that relates to the person's sense of security, self-image, or self-worth. Yes, sometimes resolution is necessary for practical reasons, so you can meet a deadline, avoid a PR problem, or make important numbers, for example. However, if you can go deeper to understand the "why" behind the conflict, try it.

"Why?" is the most important and dangerous word after "But." Ask it carefully. Simon Sinek brought a lot of attention to understanding "your why" in his book *Start With Why*[4]. In asking why, you're looking to help someone understand the meaning or motivation behind their actions, not to threaten them by putting them on the spot. It's an exploratory "why," not an inquisitor's "why."

For example, "Why" as exemplified in "Why did you do that?" provokes a defensive reaction that inhibits exploration. Alternatives like "What I was looking for was . . . " "What I still have doubts about is . . ." or mirroring a reply like "It seems like . . ." are all more effective ways to explore the question of "why" without sparking defensiveness. Some other tips for coaching through conflict:

- Some people aren't comfortable with conflict, even if it's necessary. Encouragement, listening, and understanding can help bring it out into the open and resolve it.
- Invest in the intervention, not the outcome.
- Start by establishing the things the parties can agree on and lead with the positive.
- Acknowledge all points of view. Everyone is right in his or her own mind.
- Resist the temptation to gossip.
- Keep your language neutral and calm. Not making people feel defensive is a big part of defusing conflict.

You Are the Energy Source

The great Peter Drucker said, "Your first and foremost job as a leader is to take charge of your own energy and then help to orchestrate the energy of those around you." Coaching and a coaching culture can be seen as a means for orchestrating the energy of your organization. However, that's a great deal more challenging in a WFH situation.

When everyone is in the office, we feed off each other's energy. If you define "energy" as a contagious mood, then the leader's role is to set the mood for the entire organization. Show up gloomy, and you cast a pall over your workforce. Show up buoyant and positive, and you uplift everyone. Being in a leadership role is an energy multiplier; as one person, your position gives you the power to affect the mood—the energy—of hundreds or thousands. However, in WFH, that dynamic changes.

I won't belabor the reason. Obviously, you're not present to rally the troops or radiate optimism after a tough loss. Leaders are the organization's main source of energy, and it's important to recognize that each interaction has only three possible outcomes:

- You add energy to the environment.
- You withdraw energy from the environment.
- You leave the energy level the same as when you arrived.

Remote work is inherently low-energy because we're social animals and we're unable to feed off one another's emotion, so your ability to bring energy to a remote environment is essential. People work for people, not organizations. They will always be more motivated if they're in a work environment that makes them feel good.

Leaders have to be that source of positive, affirmative energy. So how do you apply your coaching mindset and deliver the electricity your people need through MS Teams and Slack?

Remind people that you're all in this together, sharing the same adventure. Be the one who recognizes efforts before they yield results because you know they will. Celebrate small wins because you know they become transformative over time. Remind everyone what they share—a mission, the same values, goals—heck, even a sense of humor or shared memories from a company outing. Be the first to be vulnerable or self-deprecating.

Show empathy. Talk about your own anxiety and acknowledge you're still finding your own way. Try and avoid the words "no" and "but"; they shut doors instantly, so say "Yes, and" to ideas whenever you can, even just to open discussion of them. Provide the structure for people to have clear, honest exchanges about issues. Make it clear that you believe in them.

Finally, remind everyone that you expect them to be accountable, not only to you but to each other. In *The Oz Principle,* Roger Connors wrote, "Left uncorrected in an organization, victim attitudes can erode productivity, competitiveness, morale, and trust to the point that correction becomes so difficult and expensive that the organization can never fully heal itself."[5] Your people are not victims. They are powerful agents of change. It's your job as a coach to remind them of that power.

Chapter Seven

PILLAR NUMBER THREE: PEER LEARNING

Peer learning is the logical end stage of self-reflection and the coaching culture and mindset that we have already discussed. Peer learning takes the central features of reflective leadership and coaching culture and turns them loose in a welcoming, safe, hierarchy-free setting where leaders ride the bench and colleagues do the heavy lifting of listening, storytelling, and encouraging each other's growth. Equals come together to share "big talk" instead of small talk and explore shared values and interests. A community of peers lead, not the folks in the C-suite.

In a peer learning environment, every employee receives recognition and respect as a potential source of motivation and inspiration. In the work from anywhere world, where leaders are already stretched thin as they strategize ways to grow companies and continue to optimize their organizations, peers have become a critical resource. Teams and individuals continue to develop important skills, culture gains strength and depth, and this all happens organically without putting further demands on leadership. At JumpCrew, we have found peer learning invaluable.

There's often confusion between *peer learning, peer training,* and *peer onboarding,* so I'll try to clear the air. Peer training (sometimes known as *peer-to-peer learning*) is about individuals imparting specific skills to their colleagues, while peer onboarding specifically focuses on peers helping new hires acclimate to an organization. Peer learning is a method for learning via shared knowledge and community building by way of shared experience and open, heartfelt personal storytelling. Forums, whether live or online, connect people from different teams, locations, and practice areas who might otherwise only share the experience of an all-hands meeting. Connection and personal development, not merely professional development, are the end goals.

This form of peer learning requires a commitment from leadership, not from everyone in the organization. Not everyone in your org will ready and available for it, and that's okay. As you'll see, the type of peer learning I'm discussing is intimate and personal, placing it outside the comfort zone of some employees. That's normal. However, for the people who are open to it, peer learning is transformative. With executive support and enough individuals to engage, peer learning can contribute more than any other force I have ever seen to building personal connection and a vibrant, trust-rich community within an organization. Imagine leading a company where people listen to, learn from, and care about one another—even in WFH.

In WFH, the most important validation of peer learning's value is that it encourages autonomy—not just in terms of workplace decision-making but in terms of self-reflection. Working remotely, people naturally turn inward. While that can present a chance for growth for a few, for most of us, swimming in our psychic wounds and self-doubts, the isolation of WFH at times leaves us either feeling dull and soporific or lost in self-accusation and worry.

From that perspective, this value proposition lands hard:

. . . .

In WFH, peer learning creates the community that reflective leadership and coaching cannot. One-to-one bonding suffers in a WFH environment, but peer learning can help replace some of those warm, generous connections.

. . . .

How Peer Learning Works

The peer learning dynamic has two chief components:

Planning and Management. The L&D, executive, or HR Team define the goals and objectives of the program. This group is dedicated to creating the agenda and content for the meetings, getting executive support, organizing and scheduling sessions, identifying and training facilitators, monitoring facilitator and participant feedback, and organizing and managing the program.

Participation and Peer Groups. A critical mass of participants engaged and committed to showing up for all the meetings and staying focused and engaged throughout.

Peer learning groups meet in a private environment—a conference room, a Zoom call, or at JumpCrew, on the Circl.es platform—designed to foster a safe space for vulnerability, admissions of fear or failure, questions, and much more. Circl.es is built specifically for peer learning. It allows the speaker to be in the middle of the circle, lets listeners show approval without interrupting, allows facilitators to set and track a random order of speakers, and permits anyone to initiate a "group hug." There is no record button. These meetings are private.

Especially in the WFH world, tools like Circl.es has exponential power to drive culture, connections, and change in the organization. Peer learning is where people go deep, where the chemistry of risk, trust, and candor ignites to produce incredible relationships. In forum style meetings, people are asked to practice honesty and candor. These meetings are facilitated, structured conversations that ask for a commitment to truth seeking, not confirmation. The norms of many traditional corporate meetings tend to be about confirming the already-held thoughts and beliefs of the most senior member of the meeting. However, peer learning meetings set new norms as an upfront contract for the participants.

Confirmatory thought is hard to change because self-serving bias is strong, especially when others reward us and feed our ego. Truth-seeking groups discourage people from seeking evidence that supports their argument or confirms their biases and instead look to challenge preconceptions and confront difficulties in areas such as identity or self-confidence. This approach allows the participants to benefit from the hallmarks of peer learning: equality, intellectual diversity, courage to speak, and willingness to share. This lets us reframe how meetings run and turn them into experiences where truth—even disquieting or uncomfortable truth—is self-reinforcing.

Peer learning groups also commit to "norms" or rules of engagement:

1. **Commit**. Be fully present, follow the rules, be on time, listen.
2. **Contribute**. Be courageous and share, embrace vulnerability, be honest.
3. **Confide**. Trust the group and keep everything confidential.

Participants seek to become more comfortable with being uncomfortable, reinforce exploratory thought, and agree not to give advice, limiting their feedback to experience sharing, which is why this is a form of coaching.

For some employees, a peer learning forum represents their first opportunity to explore the space between giving advice/problem-solving and sharing and reflecting. Some will naturally become anxious and deeply uncomfortable. That's understandable; many people struggle with sharing their thoughts and feelings in a group and have never imagined doing so in a professional environment where they believe the ethos is to "show up, get the job done, and go home." At JumpCrew, we encourage our people to participate in forums; they certainly have the right not to.

However, after collecting years of feedback, we are convinced that these exchanges not only build crucial reservoirs of trust and deep bonds between employees who engage in them but are also incredible sources of organic learning that stick with people better and complements a well-orchestrated corporate training program or Individual Learning Plan (ILP).

So if you make peer learning part of your Accelerated Organization, know that some folks will opt out. That's okay. Your culture is your culture, and knowing who isn't able to participate or doesn't fit is valuable information. Having people refuse peer learning can serve as a flag that they might not be ready for it or ideal fits for your evolving culture in the future.

Peer Learning and WFH

Writing for sales training company Brainshark[1], Lauren Boutwell lists five reasons peer learning is essential for remote workers:

1. It replaces in-person "water cooler" talk.
2. It reinforces training.
3. It makes training programs more current.
4. It helps B and C players level up.
5. It facilitates the virtual exchange of institutional knowledge (and remote selling tips).

Peer learning formalizes the changing role of leaders in organizations where much of the workforce engages remotely. It bypasses leaders in their traditional roles in favor of work peers and colleagues interfacing directly, so the collective becomes the source of learning and enlightenment. Leaders support, facilitate, and participate with others on the same level. There's no hierarchy, which is why this serves the strategic goals of the organization. What leader wouldn't want their team to be more insightful, empowered, and self-aware?

Circl.es

At JumpCrew, we're big fans of Circl.es, so a little more detail is in order. Circl.es was founded by Dan Hoffman, an entrepreneur with years of great growth experiences in the live peer forums offered by YPO (Young Presidents Organization) and EO (Entrepreneurs Oraganzation). Both are peer groups for CEO's that have an in-person peer learning component that inspired Dan to create an online version and make it available to more than the most senior executives. It's an online environment designed to facilitate similarly impactful, non-hierarchical dialogue and sharing. In other words, it's perfect for peer learning and was designed to replicate the in-person YPO and EO forum experience.

In JumpCrew, a Circl.es session with six to eight people begins with a warm-up exercise where each person is given the floor to speak (not unlike the tradition of the "talking stick" in Native American culture). A team member in each Circle is designated as facilitator and is trained to track talk time, manage the meeting's agenda, and maintain the norms (such as "no offering advice"). The on-screen environment is literally a circle, but it's adaptive to the situation. Participant icons can converge on one person to deliver a "digital hug." Silent listeners can signal their support for what someone is saying by clicking "+1." The order of speakers can be randomized with the touch of a button, so no one stands out as a leader. Zoom is about a presentation, one to many. Circl.es is about the tribe. As Dan says, "If you want to change the world, build a tool that changes behavior. More circles, fewer rows."

The essence of a Circle is about sharing experiences around a singular content theme in an environment that provides safety and confidentiality. What happens in the Circle stays there. These are not bitch sessions. Everyone is accountable for what they share.

The object of the Circle is to bring out the best in everyone, reflecting the group's shared purpose—invitation, not confrontation. As Jonathan Hefter, Circl.es' head of program design and delivery, says, "A Circl.es journey within a company paints a picture and says 'Come meet me here.'"

The whole thing sounds like it should come with a side order of granola, right? I thought so at one point, but the power of this welcoming, naturally humanistic environment became obvious at the Aspen Institute, the famous executive leadership development program. Jonathan told me about an assembled group of high-achievers who assembled at Aspen in mid-2020 with the pandemic raging and fell in love with Circl.es because it connected them in a way they had been missing.

Forced to go virtual, they hated the experience at first but then came to realize what a marvelous equalizer it was. There were no status games; you couldn't see who flew in on a Gulfstream jet and who arrived in their Toyota Highlander. The group ended up using Circl.es three times a week, and eventually reached out to Jonathan's team and said, "Can you design the environment like we're in the woods?" They could. Not long after, you had a group of top CEOs sharing a virtual woodland, reading poetry to each other like they were putting on a college theater production of *Dead Poet's Society*. Wonderful.

Not needing to lead, not having to stand out, not trying to be the alpha dog—it's incredibly freeing. This sort of peer interaction frees you to be more of who you really are. "My circle of people has held me accountable," Jonathan says. "I listen differently to my wife because of Circl.es. If someone across the circle says, 'Just listen, don't try to fix me,' I pay attention."

The Benefits of Peer Learning

Peer learning at its core is about truth seeking. Truth seeking is different than the more typical interaction that exists to confirm your existing thoughts and beliefs. As professional poker player Annie Duke wrote in *Thinking in Bets*, "What makes a decision great is not that it has a great outcome. A great decision is the result of a good process, and that process must include an attempt to accurately represent our own state of knowledge. That state of knowledge, in turn, is some variation of 'I'm not sure.'"[2]

Self-knowledge helps us make superior decisions, but decisions become still better when tempered by the compassionate but candid feedback of a thoughtful peer group. One of the essential rules of engagement for anyone seeking truth about their own capacity owes it to themselves to explore accuracy, not confirmation. Groups have the power to reshape individual behavior by shining a light on those times we're gaslighting ourselves, avoiding a difficult issue, or looking for evidence that supports our own argument.

It's incredibly hard to see yourself from the outside in, especially when your ego and belief system don't want you to pull back the curtain. Seeing your actions without having the clarity of what you need and want can lead you to practice introspection for years without having any major breakthroughs. That's what I did. It's placebo self-awareness.

When you can open up to the reality that you might be wrong and that others might have a view of you that's more accurate than your own, you'll enjoy the real assets of a peer feedback:

- Intellectual diversity
- Courage to speak
- Willingness to share

Leaders and individual contributors who choose this route can see benefits that materially improve business-level outcomes. Imperative's 2019 Workforce Purpose Index[3], a survey of more than one thousand U.S. full-time workers, found that peer learning helps create a better work environment over the long term. According to the survey, people who regularly engage in peer coaching are 65 percent more likely to feel fulfilled at work and 67 percent more likely to be a top performer. They're also 73 percent more likely to report feeling a sense of belonging at work and about 50 percent more likely to stay in their jobs for more than five years.

Sixty-seven percent more likely to be a top performer? That means peer learning might be your best tool for turning your B players into A players, the superstars who drive most of your company's performance. There's a great deal of research to support the idea that encouraging a rich peer-led environment of confidential, intimate sharing can be the secret sauce for a great organization, remote or otherwise.

In another example, researchers from Ireland's University of Ulster looked at ten different models of peer learning—proctoring (in senior students teaching junior students), student partnerships, seminars, private study groups, peer assessments, collaborative work, mentoring, and more—and found peer learning in all forms to be a powerful but underutilized tool for growth in higher education.[4] It stands to reason the same would be true in a professional environment, whatever form your brand of peer interaction takes.

The traditional corporate mentoring structure sets managers up to fail for a simple reason: No matter what you do, your subordinates are unlikely to see you as someone who understands their struggles or with whom they can be completely candid. That's not to say that one-to-one coaching lacks value—it can be quite valuable—but it's not as effective when you use it in isolation. The peer learning environment of confidential forums and Circles gives you a second option that:

- Enables deeper connections and trust and enhances community;
- Celebrates diversity of opinion, experience, cultures, and ideas;
- Encourages open sharing and airing of issues that individuals might fear bringing up with their superiors;
- Makes everyone more receptive to new ideas and suggestions for correction; and
- Serves as an effective "pressure relief valve" for frustration, stress, and tension that might otherwise boil over publicly.

Susan Ashford, professor of management and organizations at the University of Michigan's Ross School of Business, found this to be especially true when she and her colleagues looked at the effect on various forms of collaborative peer development on people working remotely. Their work differentiates *peer learning* from *peer coaching* from *peer mentoring* (which seems to me to be *peer hair-splitting*, but I digress), but the gist of the findings was that while the isolation experienced by remote colleagues can lead to substantial increases in loneliness, irritability, anxiety, and guilt, peer learning helps employees confirm and use what they know while feeling more engaged and less stressed at work.[5]

I know this to be true from watching JumpCrew during the time that we went from a traditional "work from the office" company to a remote work org, and the NPS data we received from surveying participants was off the charts as well. People's ability to connect with each other, their comfort in sharing their authentic selves via a medium that a few months before might have seemed stilted and weird, was a key to our consistent growth during lockdown. All our people, from sales to customer support, found fairly seamless ways to be warm and open and real on an LCD flat panel and over an Internet connection—not only with each other, but with our customers. I found that quick pivot astonishing and worthy of respect, and I still do.

Deep Dive

GOOGLE'S PROJECT ARISTOTLE[6]

One of the most influential looks at the role of psychological safety in the workplace comes from those innovative geniuses at Google. Called Project Aristotle, the initiative spent two years studying 180 teams within the tech giant, trying to figure out what made some teams more effective than others.

After considering qualities like blends of backgrounds and expertise led them nowhere, the researchers found what they were looking for in the intangible "group norms" that governed how teams operated when they were together. They landed on five characteristics that were common to effective teams, the most significant being "psychological safety."

That is, as a result of norms, agreed-upon rules, and a culture where leaders signed on and people felt safe to be wrong, ask questions, take risks, and share their opinions without fear of being judged. The team became their personal safe zone where they were free to be their authentic selves, even if that authenticity meant they were strange, combative, or neurotic.

Psychological safety is what all teams strive for—what all of us desire at and away from work. As psychiatrist and author Bessel van der Kolk writes, "Being able to feel safe with other people is probably the single most important aspect of mental health; safe connections are fundamental to meaningful and satisfying lives."[7]

Psychological Safety

The linchpin to peer learning, the element that makes it go and makes it such a boon to businesses large and small, is *psychological safety*. That's the sense that you're in an environment in which you can let your guard down without fear of judgment or punishment. For some, that's our family. For others, it might be among our best friends or teammates on a sports team or, for members of the military, among their colleagues in uniform. Whatever the context, psychological safety is critical to learning and growth.

I asked Alden Mills about the importance of psychological safety. Alden is a friend and mentor—a successful entrepreneur, CEO, speaker, former Navy SEAL, and the author of several books, including *Be Unstoppable* and *Unstoppable Teams*. He knows everything there is to know about what turns a gathering of workers into a band of brothers, and he shared some of that with me.

"The work from home environment isn't one size fits all, but there's a dependency on self-discipline and self-reliance," he begins. "The leader working remotely has to make it personal. You can't go straight to the transaction. You have to do relationship building first. What is each person struggling with? Are you uncovering the struggle?

"Say it turns out that this person's discipline sucks, they get easily distracted, and they aren't good at setting their own goals, no matter what corner of their room or apartment they're working with," Alden continues. "They're really reliant on other people because they're not getting the emotional fulfillment from isolation and being by themselves. It's a spectrum, and once you start to understand where each person sits on that spectrum, you have the ability to move them from a state of selfishness.

"What I mean by that is that they might start out here: *Oh, it's all about me. Look at my life right now. This sucks. I'm having pity parties every day. My focus is only on the negative,*" he goes on. "But when the leader can come in with empathy and says, 'You're struggling here? You know what? I struggled there too. Let me show you some things that helped me.' Then the other person thinks *Oh my God, somebody really does care for me.*

"There's this point in relationships that you can move people from selfishness to selflessness," Alden concludes. "Once you can get people to start moving toward serving others, that's the magic of helping them feel valued—helping them feel like they have impact, helping them focus on something other than themselves and their own personal plight, helping them to grow the confidence to contribute at their maximum level. That's when you get that band of brothers, when they're all focused on each other, not watching their own backs."

That's a brilliant insight. Peer learning works because it's not about you. It's about everyone else. At the same time, everyone else is focused, at least in part, on your well-being. When you're confident that's the case—when you know in your heart that everyone in that tribal circle has your best interest in mind and is there to serve you, just as you're there to serve them—you have psychological safety. That's when the magic happens.

Psychological safety breeds authenticity, another of the keys to effective peer learning. When people feel like they don't have to put on a work persona, when they can be who they really are without fear, they're comfortable and open to discovery. That's especially true in WFH, when they're in their private space and *allowing the company* to temporarily co-opt that space.

But even in a peer-to-peer culture, psychological safety starts with the leader, just like everything else. Remember, culture flows downstream. "Those who hold power are obligated to do their own work, or the else members of the community bear the brunt of their toxic behavior," says Jerry Colonna. "Whether it's in the family or a corporate board room, those who hold power have to go first. By going first, they create the psychological safety that allows everybody else to do their work." They lead by example.

"If the person who holds power is not ready, then everyone will suffer," Jerry continues. "The hard fact is that most people aren't ready to grow up. If you look at statistics like the incidence of depression and anxiety in men thirty-five to sixty years old, it is partially driven by midlife transition. But it's also partially driven by the fact that we get to that age and we have never learned to deal with our feelings.

"So you have all these super successful people who lack the motivation to do their own work," Jerry concludes. "There's confirmation bias because they're successful. They hold power. That's their definition of success. I can tell you from my own work with lots and lots of rich and powerful people, that is a false definition." What remains unclear, sadly, are the limitations successful people who resist deeper reflection have placed on their own ability to achieve.

If you, the leader, are honest, open and seek self-awareness, you'll create the conditions under which people will feel safe doing the same. Whether in a group forum, deep individual reflection and learning, or in therapy, any individual's ability to achieve their fullest potential is limited by their willingness to recognize their own behavioral patterns and limitations. I have come across many "successful" people who have said they don't believe in therapy, which is another way of saying they fear self-reflection. I've heard this from people who pride themselves on their achievement but lack the courage to open the locked doors of their minds and confront what's there, and I often wonder about the toll success has taken and will take on their lives.

In this context, I don't think we can define "success" according to financial or career achievements anymore. Instead, success has to be defined as your ability to exploit your full potential as a leader and as a human being. Success is about being the best person you can be—emotionally, spiritually, intellectually, physically, in your relationships, and, yes, professionally. For the leaders I know who have found the courage to open those locked doors and confront their failures and destructive patterns, professional accomplishment comes naturally as a consequence of their personal development.

Truth Charters and Social Gatherings

Peer learning can take place in any kind of environment that offers intimacy and confidentiality. In a funny way, the urgent transition to WFH was a blessing for peer learning because no physical space could ever offer the combination of safety from viral transmission and total security and confidentiality that something like Circl.es or, to a lesser degree, a Google Meet or Zoom can offer. However, no matter where peer sessions play out, they tend to convene around a similar set of challenges and needs. Common challenges include:

- Acquiring mutual understanding;
- Finding mutual respect;
- Airing concerns or conflicts best kept confidential for the time being;
- Encouragement—a word that literally means "to give someone else courage";
- Seeking more clarity and awareness about oneself; and
- Facilitating a structured conversation that includes all participants.

In general, peer learning doesn't usually start with a fixed target. Peers come together primarily to learn what makes each other tick and to discover the wisdom of each other's experiences. Any specific takeaways that might arise from a given session are often the spontaneous result of free-form discussion facilitated by a skilled individual (more on facilitators shortly).

In other circumstances, peer learning lets the organization more deliberately tap the resources of employee's experiences by directing the discussion toward exploring specific questions or challenges. Here, the "check your ego at the door" ethos of online peer learning becomes vital because no one person is more or less important than another. Individual knowledge that might be overlooked in a traditional office environment, where it tends to be all about the leaders, is likely to get a fair hearing.

Peer learning seeks to help people become comfortable facing realities that may be disquieting, such as past failures or longtime fears. This is exceptionally useful if you're building a culture that puts a premium on candor and speaking truth. At JumpCrew, we began with a terrific idea from our director of training and development, Amber Bartlett, who we hired in March of 2020. She suggested defining the most important core competencies we were hiring for on the individual contributor and manager levels. We would then build our Circles around the development of each of those core competencies for individual contributors (our 101 content) and team leads, managers, and executives (our 201 content).

This focus brought intention to the program based on accelerating participants' ability to succeed in our environment. Here's a summary of our Circles 101 agenda:

Pre-meeting articles are links to relevant content participants can read to prep for the peer learning session, while challenge prompts give attendees something to work on after the session. Each person addresses the challenge prompt between meetings and then shares their experience the next time the group gathers.

Peer forums or gatherings can also coalesce around almost any need that's mission critical to the organization and its people:

- Communicating clearly and without misunderstanding
- Self-motivation
- Breaking isolation in WFH
- Adapting to change
- Resolving conflict
- Getting unstuck on a project
- Unstructured sharing and storytelling

The point is to promote growth and self-discovery and to feed a culture where everyone's contribution is respected. Peer learning sessions are also rich social opportunities, something everyone appreciates when they are working remotely. The dynamic in JumpCrew virtual meetings is almost always relaxed, playful, democratic, and open. People look forward to them—not because they've been told to but because regular exchanges with peers serve to deepen connections across the company and encourage collaborative problem-solving.

Circl.es fosters professional development, connects people across departments, and helps us identify and develop our next generation of leaders. Participation is a leading indicator of success and has led to increased job satisfaction score ratings and reviews. That's bottom-line value that's directly attributable to peer learning.

The Facilitator

The word *facilitator* comes from the Latin root *facil*, which means "easy." The word literally means "someone who makes things easy." A facilitator is the calm, measured, neutral party who kicks off a peer learning session, manages norms, and "holds space" for conversation, sharing, and vulnerability to occur. The facilitator is a key figure in a group peer learning environment, making sure everyone feels heard and recognized. If they've done their job well, all participants spoke in even amounts and the conversation flowed at the right pace.

In all circles, regardless of online, in-person, or tech platform, facilitators are particularly pivotal. Their primary job is to manage the flow of the agenda—the work to be done, the challenges or questions that get people talking—and then to get out of the way. As Jonathan Hefter wrote on the JumpCrew facilitator Slack channel:

> A huge part of effective facilitation is uncovering the real work. As the Facilitator, modeling vulnerability is a shortcut to getting at what really needs addressing. Consider sharing first in the challenge round, or asking the first

probing question, to consistently set the tone for the meeting, and drive to the challenge underneath what's shared. Are they listening, or are they checking their email?

Being able to read the room will make you a better Facilitator, manager, and coworker. Learn to notice. To sense and respond to what's happening in the room, rather than blindly driving the agenda. If folks are multi-tasking, it says as much about your effectiveness in enforcing the norms as it does about the participants. If no one has a thoughtful question for the challenge presenter, perhaps you haven't encouraged the presentation to end with a question. Maybe it wasn't the most appropriate challenge to choose as the day's presentation. Or maybe you've allowed a tone of lethargy to infect the meeting.

Your work as a facilitator and leader is to discover your work and then with all your heart and effort to give it to yourself. Also consider the level of compassion you demonstrate—difficulty in sharing more deeply can stem from years of being cut off or not being allowed to express an opinion.

What makes a great facilitator? First, understanding the distinction between facilitating and leading. Executives and leaders are used to doing all the talking. Facilitators are like the narrators at the beginning of a story: they set the stage and then get out of the way. They lead from the side. A good rule of thumb is that if you speak more than 30 percent of the time during a session with more than four people, you need to recalibrate either your participation or what you're saying to get other people to speak up. As Dan Hoffman says, "Facilitating is about your intention when you enter the room."

With remote work in some form doubtless here to stay, facilitating is coming to be regarded as a mission-critical skill set. They are not the masters of ceremonies but more lion tamers, adept at bringing groups together to tackle thorny subjects and serving as traffic cop to ensure every idea is heard and everyone given equal time to contribute.

Writing in *Fast Company*, Brandon Klein, partner at the Difference Consulting, describes facilitators as the people who break meetings free of the dreaded agenda-driven death march and turn them into free-flowing idea sessions that can flex to the immediate demand. "As the general population diversifies, so will the workplace of the future, and forward-looking companies are already hard at work to actively diversify their ranks," he writes. "People with different backgrounds and points of view chipping away at the same problem together are more likely to reach creative solutions. But it isn't inevitable that they'll do so all on their own, without a facilitator to guide things. One reason facilitation is becoming an even more important job skill going forward is because organizations will need people who know how to harness all that diversity of thought and channel it productively."[8]

FACILITATORS:

- Manage and optimize the time and agenda, including making sure everyone gets equal airtime, and are sensitive to time when people are sharing deeply;
- Set the mood;
- Model ideal temper and behavior for the room, virtual or otherwise;
- Provide positive reinforcement for someone who might be reluctant to open up or dig into difficult material;

- Listen far more than they speak;
- Repeat important points so they're not missed;
- Reflect with group on important points;
- Generate opening questions and talking points; and
- Find the key "why" in the conversation.

However, the chief job of a facilitator is to foster and maintain psychological safety. He or she is the person emphasizes the importance of showing up on time, holds people accountable for adhering to the norms, and contributes meaningfully. The facilitator opens the door for conversation, often leading the meeting a warm-up exercise like the "weather report" (asking each attendee to describe their own internal weather) or the six-word story, which is self-explanatory.

Peer learning groups help people distinguish between their thoughts, feelings, and facts, so they come to understand that their thoughts and feelings are not facts. It's about encouraging everyone to face hard truths about themselves, even in the face of discomfort in sharing personal thoughts and feelings in a group. Exploration, even if you're not crazy about the answers, is the goal. Peer learning creates a safe space where good things happen. This is a transformational tool that relatively few organizations are leveraging, which means it could offer a major competitive edge for your organization as you work to develop a more self-aware, bonded, thoughtful workforce.

Chapter Eight

PEER LEARNING AND THE BOTTOM LINE

Perks, those pleasurable extras that make the team smile and make work feel less like work, have always been essential parts of building a workplace culture. Perks became infamous and sometimes excessive during the dotcom boom, and even in what feels like the long-ago era before COVID-19, perks might have meant extras like nap rooms, gourmet cafeterias where all meals were free, morning yoga classes, and roving masseurs. Companies like Google spent small fortunes on onsite childcare, movie field trips, and "bring your dog to work" days. Even small startups gave their people unlimited free gourmet coffee and foosball in the break room, and it seemed more like a requirement as the competition for talent increased.

I'm not saying that stuff doesn't matter because I'm all for wellness perks. But in the WFH era, those goodies have lost a great deal of their luster. Instead, when so many people put in some or all of their hours from their kitchen tables, the new perk is *people*. That's right, say goodbye to Free Beer Fridays and hello to human contact.

People in a WFH situation appreciate warm, genuine interactions, making peer learning the foundation for a vibrant organizational culture. Alden Mills, whom you heard from in the previous chapter, told me about one of his consulting clients, a large telecom company that is leveraging WFH to strengthen the bonds between its people and achieve greater alignment between individual contributors and leadership's vision. "They are all in alignment with the company's cultural values," he said in our interview. "They're using this time as a springboard to build even greater trust, get more creative, and do more things. They've realized that now people have more time, so they're encouraging them to set agendas and create their own virtual little breakout rooms. They're getting so much more done. They're soaring."

It also helped that this company gave each of its twenty thousand employees a thousand-dollar check to help them set up their home offices. Knowing that lines during the 2020 election would be long, they gave each employee six hours of paid time to vote so they wouldn't need to take PTO. Now, steps like that take some substantial resources that not all organizations have, but the substance of those acts wasn't really the money or the time. It was the commitment and the trust. Those traits come to the fore naturally in an organization where peer learning, community, and respect flourish.

Taking the Granola Out of Peer Learning

If you Google information about peer learning, it isn't exactly what I've described: a hierarchy-free gathering space whose primary goal is to be a welcoming, open forum for sharing stories, confronting uncomfortable truths, and growing in self-awareness. Instead, the phrase "peer-to-peer learning" is common and seems to denote something more like "peer training," a more reductive, goal-driven type of interaction, where peers come together to develop specific skill sets ranging from software applications to time management or conflict resolution. "Peer-to-peer onboarding" is another popular iteration.

There's nothing wrong, of course, with peer interaction designed as a substitute for a more traditional training format or for an inspiring employee handbook and a rote HR lecture for a new hire. In fact, such learning might be an asset to organizations worried about retaining their best people as the post-COVID economy gathers steam. In 2019, payroll giant ADP cited peer-to-peer learning as one of the ways that "organizations with limited operational budgets and manpower (can) build a culture of innovation that helps them get the most out of their workforce"[1] and retain their best talent. It's easy to imagine that the same is true today.

However, the tactical, training-oriented type of peer learning is not one of the Three Pillars. In the kind of remote organization that becomes a community, everything begins with self-reflection, personal growth, and a willingness to share. Peer learning allows the organization to take on a more open-ended, open-minded form in which real emotions, small epiphanies, and community building take priority over developing hard or easily quantifiable workplace skills. While that might sound innovative and appealing, the approach also raises concerns that "peer learning JumpCrew style" ignores the bottom line and practicality in favor of feel-good vibes.

Nothing could be further from the truth. Yes, the type of peer learning we're talking about here is holistic and humanistic, built on questions and honest, personal exploration of the answers. But one look at the data tells you that growth opportunities and the chance to be present with people they care about are exactly what employees crave, especially in remote work. Mercer's 2020 Global Talent Trends report found, among many other fascinating tidbits, that half of employees (49 percent, to be exact) prefer to work in an organization that prioritizes employee health and well-being, and 71 percent want a midlife checkup for health, wealth, and career.[2]

In other words, perhaps more than ever before, employees are looking to their employers for more than foosball and ping pong. And while so-called "upskilling" or "reskilling" (as Mercer's report calls it) is also a vital part of learning and development in any evolving organization in the WFH world, it's soft, personal qualities like empathy and attention to employees' holistic well-being that help individual contributors feel they are respected and regarded as mission-critical members of the tribe.

Personal growth through reflection and self-discovery isn't work masquerading as a therapy session. Peer learning is purposeful, channeled growth with a team objective: to help individuals work past their predisposed answers, their internal conflicts, and their fears to clearly see their full capacity as human beings. Who wouldn't want a company filled with people working at being their best? With that kind of whole-person development in the rear-view mirror, employees are more ready to learn and level up new skills because they've let go of much of what was holding them back.

That's why there's no contradiction between peer learning (or any of the pillars) and building the most valuable organization. I'm a capitalist and an entrepreneur. I believe in the profit motive. I just happen to believe, based on my own experiences and the wisdom of many others, that sustainable growth, profitability, and long-term value is served by helping your people show up every day feeling empowered and appreciated and being part of a caring community committed to becoming better versions of themselves.

Organizations can be fiercely driven and deeply reflective at the same time. In fact, when you combine the relentless drive to build, grow, scale, and monetize with the value created when your team has the structure and makes time to reflect be thoughtful, and become more aware, the business and businesspeople are better for it.

Autonomy and the "Commander's Intent"

One of the signal traits of peer learning that make it most valuable is also the one that can make it most challenging to leaders: *autonomy*. Yes, ideally peer learning sessions are led by a skilled facilitator, but what's just as important is who's not in your circle or forum: *your boss*. The facilitator maintains the norms and ensures talk time is respected, but otherwise, nobody's in charge. The C-suite's agenda is not in play. Control over what occurs in these sessions is *passive* and arises from the norms you establish and the culture that drives your organization.

As uncomfortable as it might seem not to have direct control over the conversation in a peer learning circle, this activity builds the autonomy that's so important in WFH. As I said earlier, empathy can be a trap when it stops a leader from holding a person on the team accountable. Autonomy is the fix. When people feel responsible for their own direction and growth, they're far more likely to be accountable and less likely to fumble a goal they've set for themselves.

The key? As Alden Mills says, it's setting your "commander's intent"—modeling and promoting an organizational culture that represents the work you'd like to see done. "At the end of the day, in a work from home environment, you're pushing," Alden says. "It's just like being in special operations. You're sending people far down range, far away from other bases. You have to trust them to make the decisions with the commander's intent, but they may get there in multiple different ways. The organizations that are going to struggle are the ones with the largest gap between the actual and the aspirational values of their business—the ones that have been lying to themselves and saying, 'Oh, this is our culture here, our core values, you know, etched in stone, somewhere that no one has ever seen.'"

Alden's point is that WFH reveals the gap between the actual and aspirational values of your organization. Before WFH became a mandate, most leaders said all the right things about trust and giving their people autonomy. Because times were busy and demanding, no one called out the ones who didn't make the investment in their community. But now, with everyone captain of his or her own little ship, those minor flaws become major ones. Companies whose individual contributors haven't learned how to bond, teach each other, and collaborate independently are finding themselves at a competitive disadvantage.

"That's one of the biggest challenges with the command-and-control, hierarchical organization," says Alden. "The power's up here and it trickles down and we tell you what to do. But that's now flipped. It's exactly what happened in special forces. In *Team of Teams* by General Stanley McChrystal, he has a moment when he realized, 'My God, I am actually the choke point. I'm the one that's saying go or no go to every mission. No wonder we're only doing a couple of missions a month when we need to be doing a couple of missions a night.' He ended up pushing decision-making down about seven levels, which was my level.

"That is saying, 'I trust you to know the commander's intent and make the right decision,'" Alden continues. "Now go forth and kick ass. That's what is happening in the work environment, whether you like it or not. You have to give away your power to empower others. A lot of egos don't like the idea of giving up something they've worked really hard for, because they're not getting the fact that it's actually going to be a boomerang for them. They don't get the fact that the more they empower their people, the more those people are going to come back to help."

The commander's intent is the culture of your organization, the values and priorities visible every day. They begin with you and other leaders.

Keeper of the Cultural Flame

Nobody is really an expert in adapting to a world where everyone is working from their spare bedroom. We trained in a very different operating environment, and we're inventing these new organizational dynamics on the fly. However, what is clear from my experience with JumpCrew is that maintaining a strong organizational community in a remote work scenario is easier when employees enjoy increased autonomy and self-determination.

Think of UPS drivers. They're given ten hours' worth of packages to deliver in eight hours, and consequently, they are endlessly hustling and reinventing ways to do their job and shave time. Organizations that push achievement are never complacent and rarely as reflective as they should be. With the "stretch goals" we set for the people we bring into JumpCrew (not to mention the goals they set for themselves), it's less likely that they're going to prioritize time for self-reflection without leaders encouraging them to do so. Instead, they're seeing the next performance target in front of them and thinking about how quickly they can pull the trigger and hit that target. They're wondering if they have the right ammo and the right gun. They're thinking at a tactical level because that's their mission and they're trying to survive.

One primary role for the leader in peer learning is to champion a culture in which employees are encouraged to carve out time to slow down, reflect, and ask hard questions. That's essential for mental and emotional well-being, but it's also a sound strategic choice because the individual gains perspective, the ability to reflect, and is able to connect meaningfully with colleagues and teammates. As the leader, it's your job to make it clear through your words and actions that such reflective pauses aren't about dodging accountability but are in fact *desirable* because they help people learn and perform their jobs better. In other words:

We don't learn from experience; we learn from reflecting on it.

But the adoption of peer learning is most likely to become widespread when leaders consistently weave its core elements—reflection, truth-seeking, vulnerability, honesty over bias, safety—into the organization's culture. You do that with your words and actions. How you encourage employees to invest their time with your own participation in peer learning and with the behaviors you incentivize.

With JumpCrew, my aggressive advocacy of peer learning

helped our people push past their early disquiet with the format and the intimacy of baring their souls to people they barely knew. In a rare demonstration of top-down leadership, we introduced the mission-critical component of peer learning into JumpCrew's docket of regular activities, making it a priority in our efforts to grow and maintain our culture in WFH. Now, Circles and the bonds that have taken root around them have built a peer learning culture that's self-sustaining and dovetails perfectly with our other programs for individual contributors and leaders. I don't think I could slow it down even if I wanted to . . . and I don't want to. It's been too good for our bottom line.

Targeted Growth

In small organizations like JumpCrew, C-level leaders can afford to take point in promoting peer learning, sometimes through their own participation. That's what I did to get the ball rolling. But in larger orgs, it's an opportunity for HR leaders to distinguish themselves. That's what's been happening at companies like Uber and Siemens, which have embraced WFH as part of their long-term plans. Ryan Golden writes in *HR Dive*:

> At Uber Freight, HR leaders have taken advantage of online channels such as chat rooms and video conferencing to create spaces in which employees can learn from one another, Contreras said. Platforms like Slack, Zoom and Degreed allow the company to place learners in breakout rooms, where there has been strong participation in smaller conversations, before returning to a larger central channel. This can also have the effect of leveling the playing field

for participation, compared to live meetings that require workers to speak up or raise hands.[3]

This account highlights one of the real benefits of conducting peer learning using the tools of remote work: the ability to create customized environments where people can feel safe, connect with other people, and interact with small groups as a key part of healthy workplace socialization. The story highlights ways that quiet Uber employees have become more outspoken over time because interaction via the Internet lets them develop in a more controlled ecosystem. This creates an interesting inversion: while WFH might be a hardship for natural extroverts, it can turn out to be a windfall for introverts.

Jarron Vosburg, a JumpCrew VP whom you met a while ago, agrees with this assessment of tech-centric WFH interaction. "It creates a more accessible environment," he says. "When you've got one hundred and thirty people sitting in a room and someone asks a question, it just feels strange to try to contribute in that environment. Virtually, it's easier to contribute because it feels like you're having an across-the-table conversation with your CEO. That's when the light switch clicked and I realized like this is probably the most powerful use of this time that we could possibly have—not only as an organization, but to demonstrate a commitment to facilitating a conversation. Creating connections around non-performance-based conversations in the virtual world can feel much more comfortable to everyone except extroverts—and we're in our own houses, in the most comfortable place, in a much more accessible platform through a screen share."

The irony of remote work may be that with its emphasis on individuality and privacy and being accessible from anywhere, it's the best environment imaginable for evoking the full potential of peer learning. While the peer learning model might be centered on personal growth, it's targeted growth with a strategic purpose.

It's a cliché, but our people are really our greatest asset, and accelerated growth in revenues and market share is only possible when our people experience accelerated growth in their ability to adapt to new situations or bounce back from failure. In other words, character and not simply skills from a resume determine the future of our business. The same is true for your business.

You Are the Safe Space

In the end, though, promoting peer learning is about your desire to champion it. In this WFH adventure, we are creating new best practices, and someone has to be responsible for saying, "This is reality and worth the risk of time and money." Leaders define reality for their organizations, even when those people are scattered across time zones.

As a leader, your other primary role here is to create a safe space for peer learning to take hold by engaging in it yourself—by participating in forums with peers and subordinates, sharing your story, and challenging your own biases and fears. It's like tilling the soil, planting a crop, and watering. As I've worked to instill the pillars of self-reflection, coaching, and peer learning in JumpCrew, I've had to be patient, especially as key players have changed, and let them grow on their own. That has been effort wisely withheld. By giving key new managers time to digest, adapt to, and ultimately adopt our culture, we let peer learning take root by allowing new managers to participate in it. I've watched the people given the time to embrace it deliver a new, dynamic kind of leadership.

Peer learning acknowledges that as leaders, we have only so much influence on how our team develops. Management theory suggests that we can shape who people become within the organization, but that's simply not true. That's someone's ego talking. We can guide, share, point the way, provide resources, support, lead by example, and reward behavior we like while sanctioning behavior we don't, but the individual chooses.

Our role as leaders is to help people see choices more clearly, with better context and information, so they can make decisions that serve themselves and our businesses at the same time. Team leads who recognize that their bosses spend more time listening than talking also learn to respond to debate patiently and thoughtfully, and are less prone to reflexively shutting down opinions they disagree with. Individual contributors who want to be more decisive and action-oriented can release the fears that are blocking that action. In the peer learning environment, while there might not be a hierarchy, some people will still rise to the top and stand out as future leaders. Some might leave the organization if they decide it's not what they want, but the ones who stay make us stronger.

You Can Only Choose Actions, Not Results

Still, you will invest time and resources in peer learning only to see some of your bravest, most insightful people leave for greener pastures once they feel they can learn or earn more elsewhere. It's frustrating, but that's a leadership lesson in not clutching outcomes too closely.

Use your bully pulpit to model the qualities you want peer learners to develop—at JumpCrew those are humility, vulnerability, transparency, mindfulness, openness, courage—and the role you want them to play as teachers and mentors. That is a big part of the effort to build community and keep it together. Higher pay? More perks? Maybe, but people stay when the opportunity feels right and go when they think the opportunity will feel better elsewhere. When an organization retains a key contributor over the long term, they make a habit of showing through actions that they value their contribution, wisdom, independent thought, and individuality. They walk their talk. Peer learning encourages participants to be authentically who they are and connect with each other. Show your best people that you value who they are, and you're more likely to keep them in the fold.

This is another example of Annie Duke's "think in bets" approach, which I mentioned in the previous chapter. In peer learning, as in poker, you can control your inputs and your environment, but the outcome is still out of your hands. As she aptly says in her book, "You can make a good decision and have a bad outcome and you can make a bad decision and get lucky." You have to decouple the decision from the outcome and accept that sometimes it mostly works out, and sometimes it doesn't. Sometimes, peer learning shines the spotlight on terrific people who stay in your company. Other times, the facilitator misses the mark, or some in the circle are not committed and fail to show up, so you end up with perplexed new hires. Shit happens.

The notion that outcomes are out of our control is an idea with its roots in Buddhism, but it's appealing if you're a leader trying to free yourself of the burdensome idea that every result depends on you. It doesn't. One of the best metaphors for this is the idea that you can't lose twenty pounds (if you wanted to). Now, that seems wrong, but unpack it. You can't simply snap your fingers and be twenty pounds lighter, can you? All you can do is make choices that you hope will change behaviors and lead to a desired outcome—working out, eating less, and so on. The outcome will be what it is.

That may be unacceptably hands-off to a confident leader schooled in command and control, but it dovetails elegantly with the outcomes of peer learning and what the millennial workforce appreciates. All you can do is be the keeper of your organization's culture and model the value of peer engagement and sharing. You can build initiatives around it, reward people for participating in it, and lean on it for mentoring and onboarding of new hires. The outcome is out of your hands. That's freeing, in a way.

Stepping-Stones to Building Community

The other important thing to remember about peer learning is that it's not isolated from the other pillars of reflective leadership and coaching culture. In fact, they might not even be pillars but feedback loops that interconnect and lead forward and back, one reinforcing the others. As a reflective leader, you learn to coach yourself, and as a peer learner you learn to be more reflective. As you improve your coaching skills, you become a better facilitator in formal and informal peer learning.

Beginning with reflective leadership, it's all about you as the leader seeing your own actions and motivations and how you build relationships with other people. Then we progress to coaching, where becoming the coach of yourself is as vital as handing off responsibility to others. However, the leader is still straddling that line. The leader is always in coaching mode by virtue of the position, and the responsibility for outcomes is split between you and the people you're coaching.

Then there's peer learning, where leaders encourage groups of people connected not by team but by community to grow autonomously in a safe environment. But even while peer learning is going on, what quality is most valuable? *Reflection*. So we circle back to the beginning, and the whole thing starts again.

Built on these three disciplines, the community draws on the natural desire and drive we all have to prove ourselves worthy to those we care about. Everything in this kind of organization encourages growth by coaxing people out of their comfort zones and rewards growth with praise, respect, and belonging. Performance rises, and the rewards become material—as a sense of accomplishment and satisfaction complement higher pay, advancement, and so on.

As long as you can find ways to appeal to that innate desire to feel worthy and to belong to something bigger than oneself, you can keep people walking those stepping-stones for years, and when they finally step off, you'll have plenty more following behind them, learning the same lessons of humility, authenticity, and accountability.

Implementing Peer Learning in WFH

Building a peer learning program is easier in a WFH organization, not only because technology like Circl.es makes it easy but because remote work creates individual "spaces" built for confidential sharing and communication. When we first introduced the JumpCrew program in 2018, we worked from offices in Nashville, New York, and Los Angeles, and it led to the comical misadventure of sixty people who worked in one open space all competing for a private space to talk from at the same time. But to implement a peer learning *culture* that's about growth and honesty, not merely learning skills, you'll need to take some specific steps:

Repeat Yourself. As your organization grows, its culture will grow only grow if you continue to spread it with the same passion you did when you were a startup. Your *memes*—the individual ideas that represent the specific values and traits you've chosen to be at the heart of your company—will carry the meaning of your culture to everyone who comes into contact with it. For example, the memes of your organization's culture might be *diversity, innovation,* and *family.* Once you know what your organization stands for, communicate those memes constantly in every possible way. The faster you grow, the more you dilute your culture. New hires can't recall the passionate younger leader delivering the all-hands message to the team of twenty all around one big table. The message you deliver today is all they ever know. No one ever lost a great employee by communicating too much. Rob and I still meet all new hires, individual contributors, and managers to deliver our cultural and leadership message firsthand. Making your cultural memes visible and audible will make it clear to everybody what values you care about. No one will be surprised when they show up in your peer learning.

Embrace Facilitator Training. Great facilitators are made, not born. Extroverted leaders naturally tend to take over the conversation and dominate the room, but that's not the facilitator's job. His or her job is to manage a great meeting. Set the scene for open, honest exchange, ensure equal opportunity talk time, and manage the agenda so things end on time. Facilitator skills require training, and without it, the risk of a poorly facilitated and unsatisfying forum runs high. So make sure you and anyone else you expect to be a facilitator receive training from a firm experienced facilitator. Don't improvise.

Establish Ground Rules. Peer learning isn't as freeform as you might think. The way we do it at JumpCrew, there is a more formal structure behind the forums. This creates a boundary of sorts where people feel safe. The ground rules or "norms" and the agenda give you the best opportunity to create meaningful learning experiences. You can compare the experience to producing a Hollywood movie. The production process is quite rigid, and producers expect the talent and crew to adhere to it. However, within the bounds of that structure, they are free to be as creative as they like.

> When you establish a code of conduct for peer learning, you ensure that interactions are timely, positive, and productive. Remember, you're looking to create an atmosphere in which people feel safe to share their stories, fears, and failures and to receive constructive feedback.

Get a Good Mix. Peer learning the way we do it at JumpCrew can be a bit overwhelming for newcomers. We blend experienced facilitators, peer learning veterans, and a sprinkling of new faces in each session. This brings some fresh energy while also including people who know the ground rules and can keep things moving. You can also match complimentary personalities—quiet with quiet, funny with funny—although sometimes, that creates a level of comfort that's counterproductive. When in doubt, lean a little toward the provocative, but not too far.

Sell It. Make sure your people know that peer learning sessions exist, when they are, and how to sign up for them and locate them online. Again, WFH makes this easier—no booking conference rooms and the like. You can run unlimited peer learning get-togethers with broadband and a subscription to Circl.es (and to a lesser degree with Zoom or Google Meet).

Finding Fit

Peer learning can take time to nurture within an organization, but once it is well established as a cornerstone of your culture, it also serves as an effective litmus test for people who are a questionable fit for the organization.

If you fully embrace the tenets I'm talking about here, you'll want to recruit individual contributors and leaders who are open to self-reflection, coaching, and other foundational principles. Peer learning sessions, steeped as they are in personal openness and vulnerability, may prove to be a bridge too far for some. There's nothing wrong with that, and it's valuable to recognize it.

Eventually, you will learn to spot individuals likely to be open to peer learning in the hiring process. That is how your organization can build a culture and community that serves everyone, from new hires to the oldest veterans.

Chapter Nine

HIRING FOR THE WFH WORLD

In my twenties, my choices led me on a career path that prioritized my desire to have fun, so I moved to California. I was going to be an entrepreneur, or so I decided when I couldn't get a career-oriented job. Lacking in focus and determination, I certainly wouldn't have succeeded in a job at JumpCrew. I was living in Los Angeles and struggling to get my career on track. While bartending in Venice Beach, I had the idea for a personal valet business. I had teed up all my contractors, came up with my marketing and advertising strategy, and I was actually the first one in the space. My buddy Howard, who had been Phi Beta Kappa at Yale and already had a successful business, was helping me. I was twenty-three years old.

Opening weekend came. My advertising was dropping, and I had my dedicated phone line set up. I had built a trusted network of contractors and told them to expect the phone to be ringing off the hook. Then, just before the weekend, I got an invitation to go on this crazy ski trip. I asked my friend Nicole to cover the phones, dropped everything, and went skiing. I don't know what the hell I was thinking.

Was it some crazy act of self-sabotage? I don't know. What I do know is that I came back to my now-defunct business and angry clients whose requests went unfulfilled and would never come back. It turned out that Nicole, who was supposed to manage the business in my absence, went to the racetrack to place a bunch of bets for someone who paid her more money than I did. Irresponsibility breeds irresponsibility, I suppose.

I had the freedom to make a choice, and I made a stupid one. I made multiple stupid ones. But that's hardly unique to me. There isn't an entrepreneur out there who hasn't done something that, when they look back, they can't believe they were dumb enough to do. But the reason I'm sharing that story is that it's an illustration of a simple truth: success is often a matter of putting the right people with the right level of maturity and experience in the right position at the right time. That's why, when it comes to building a successful, sustainable, resilient organization in a world where WFH has become the new normal, hiring the right people is more critical than ever.

A Post-Resume World

I'm not claiming that training and experience aren't important because we know they are. In running JumpCrew and my other companies, I've become persuaded that a person's ability to see themselves clearly is as important as intelligence, education, or even attitude in determining how they adapt and how far they will go. If a candidate for a position can't be honest with me when I ask about their weaknesses in an interview, then they're unlikely to admit them after they are hired. They're unlikely to grow in our organization before they fail.

In the same vein, if that same person grew up with a sense of entitlement that exceeded their desire to prove themselves, how will they contribute to making their team or our community better? Will they be a giver or taker? As my very wise eighty-seven-year-old therapist once said to me, "Without a little fire in your belly, what difference are you going to make in the world?" Years later, that fire in the belly—otherwise known as grit—would become a cornerstone of JumpCrew's cultural values. If you don't have that fire in your program when you get here, you're not likely to find it when you're under pressure to perform, particularly in an achievement-based organization.

Once upon a time, I was having lunch with a new friend, a real estate professional named Long Doan. He had an extraordinary life story. He had escaped from Vietnam at age thirteen in a boat, alone. His father spent years in a Communist reeducation camp, but that thirteen-year-old refugee has become a successful entrepreneur in Minnesota, owner of one of the largest independent real estate firms in the state. During that lunch, Long told me that there are three ways you learn: imitation, experience, and reflection—reflection being the hardest.

That's why I've focused so strongly on reflection in this book, not to mention coaching and peer learning, which aid self-reflection and self-awareness. Reflection is what separates random actions and undesirable outcomes from intentional action and desired outcomes. The combination of grit, humility, the ability to be reflective, and openness to learning are the most important qualities I look for in hiring people who can thrive in a demanding, intense, accountable environment. I'm not after checks on a resume. The hunger to learn, the willingness to say "I don't know," and to share and connect and grow are the qualities you should be looking for in the people you recruit as well.

I've written about our first hiring binge—one hundred people in one hundred days. Well, we weren't targeting the top of the class at Vanderbilt. That's just not who we are. We hire many folks from UT and Middle Tennessee State. Why? Because people don't go to college to be salespeople. They become salespeople when they need to make a living. Only then do they discover that sales is the greatest business classroom on the planet, not to mention a career most accessible to liberal arts graduates with the right qualities.

We rarely hire recent graduates. We prefer to hire people who've already had a few learning moments in the world of work. When we do hire recent grads, we look closely at their level of intrinsic motivation. We hire doers, not necessarily the best students. We're looking for bold thinkers and leaders—on teams, in communities, in their side job, or in their own journeys. We hire based on how we think people will contribute when they're on the right team, not based on their LinkedIn profile. In a lot of other organizations, the goal of leadership is to be comfortable, retain your job, look good, and get promoted. That isn't what we're after at JumpCrew, especially after the world changed and everyone was suddenly working at home.

Eddie Moncayo, JumpCrew's VP of talent acquisition, says that getting to post-resume thinking was a heavy lift at first. "We're supposed to be in a post-resume world, and that includes the hang-ups that we have reviewing a person's LinkedIn profile," he says.

"We comb over every detail, often obsessing over what the content means, and make snap judgments that instantly cancel that individual's opportunity to become a member of our team. We did a lot of work this year on selecting competencies that speak to the behaviors that we'd like our team members to have reflected in their daily work. When we've honed in on those behaviors, the issue of character and grit rises to the surface and provides us a look into what it means to be that person and whether they would translate well into our environment."

We were trying to create the chemistry to both accelerate achievement and maintain a sense of safety for taking risk and failure. We wanted our people to be challengers, to be comfortable being uncomfortable so they could grow as leaders, to connect to each other, and to become part of our community. Even as things evolve from a forced WFH scenario to something more flexible and customized, the lesson Rob and I learned during 2020 remains just as clear as ever:

. . . .

In building a high-achieving WFH organization,
hiring is the key to success.

. . . .

In the WFH world, it's not just traditional leadership skills that have become obsolete. The qualifications that might make someone a perfect hire for a face-to-face office are staggeringly different from those that make someone a great fit for a WFH organization. When you hire from a pool of folks who've been in the workforce for ten, twenty, or thirty years, they bring their programs and bias to your company. Your recruitment team's responsibility is to recognize who possesses the personal characteristics that you're looking for—and to recognize that regardless of someone's accomplishments, you can't change them.

If someone is not a fit for your culture, it doesn't matter what their list of accomplishments looks like. This is a hard lesson we've learned at JumpCrew, and it's been a limiting factor in our ability to grow by hiring experienced talent. The forced WFH experiment has exposed that truth in the starkest terms.

In any company, there's a tension between the reality of the labor pool and your aspirations. It's appealing to think of effortlessly hiring three hundred people who are reflective, humble learners with the ability to lead and the character to leave their egos out of leadership, but those recruits are not hanging out in your lobby. They're being scooped up by other companies, and that activity is only accelerating with the move to WFH. That's why some of our most talented salespeople are on the recruitment team: we know everything depends on hiring people who can thrive working remotely.

The autonomy, isolation, distractions, and complexity of remote work strip away all pretension about who fits into an organization that depends on a mostly distributed labor force. Some people, despite their experience and skills, simply cannot be effective and productive working at a distance. In part, that's because without the usual workplace dynamics and without the motivation of peers and a boss in the room, success in WFH hinges more on the qualities we've talked about here: intrinsic motivation, focus, discipline, coachability, accountability, and humility.

I asked Jarron Vosburg what else differentiates hiring for WFH from hiring for an in-person org. Systemic WFH is so new there are no hard and fast rules. However, one phenomenon he and I have both noticed is that the people who fit the 2020/2021 version of

JumpCrew are often not polished and may have resumes that have nothing to do with sales, but they are a fit because of their *character*. Character seems to be the new killer app in WFH, which makes sense. After all, I can teach someone skills, but I can't teach them to love working hard or to show up with integrity.

Example: I had a wonderful onboarding Circles call with seven new "Crewbies," and one guy's only prior experience was being a personal trainer. He was an athlete who worked hard and trained to become better and had helped others do the same. He'd never had another job, period! Well, he actually turned out to be wonderful. But he had his baseball hat on during the meeting, his camera angle was weird, and he looked like he was sitting in a Mexican restaurant for the call. Yeah, he needed some coaching. I Slacked him and had a five- or ten-minute phone call with him afterward, and I took a chance on him because things are different now.

Professionalism. Experience. Polish. We may have to tear up the recruitment rulebook for the new WFH world. Because the people who thrive and become A players in this environment will be nothing like the stars we've tried to hire in the past. If you're going to build an accelerated achievement team, you'll need more of them.

The Importance of Training in WFH

A while back, I mentioned the need for training on soft skills in peer learning, but training truly comes to the head of the class when we're talking about making new hires successful. Can you train people on your organization's culture? The answer turns out to be a qualified "yes." I spoke with Amber Bartlett and Eddie Moncayo about this and other WFH training-related questions.

"We've done a great job with product training," Amber says,

There was no decrease in the quality of people's skillsets. People were still able to meet their quotas. What we were really struggling with, though, was culture—getting people to have that same vibe that we've really loved at JumpCrew. That's been something that we've had to be much more cognizant of. We've created several events to help people still have that feeling, but we're still learning. We're hoping that as we continue to create more engagement with the CultureCrew team that plans events, having something once a month that people can participate in virtually, that we'll continue to increase engagement. But right now, it just feels like people are really close to their own team.

Amber also makes the point that when you're trying to grow culture, leadership buy-in is critical. "If you're going to do something remotely, it's much more difficult to get people involved without hearing from leadership," she says. "You can have thirty minutes in the middle of a work week to do something fun with your peers, but what I know from experience is that you have to be extremely aggressive in pushing a remote opportunity or else you just don't get people involved. We have to train up the folks in the culture and teach them that you can't just make one Slack invite about an event. You have to reach out to people. You've got to be aggressive in your Slack or email. So you've got to cast a really wide net and really push hard."

Eddie came from a previous role with a larger company where most of the workforce was remote, and that showed him that in WFH, leaders just have to accept that some people won't participate, and they need learn how to help them develop despite this. "I've had remote teams now for fifteen years at least, and there are some remote employees who don't necessarily want to participate in culture stuff," he says. "They're different animals. Often as a leader, we say that you can't cater to everybody, but in some ways you have to because you have to learn how to figure out how to connect with all different types of personalities in a remote space."

As Amber points out, leading in this manner requires a level of mindfulness that some leaders have never been called on to show. "Leaders have to be incredibly thoughtful," she says.

> Do you have an individual development plan for them? I think every single person deserves an IDP. Everybody deserves the ability to grow a technical skill and a competency. I encourage every single leader to sit down with their folks and find out what motivates them, what they're naturally good at, and then discuss a business case for how they can grow. That requires a lot of time and a lot of thoughtfulness. Making that switch from being someone whose main job is getting rid of obstacles to actively reaching out to each one of your employees takes a lot of time. It's just a different leadership skill set.

Eddie's view is a bit different, which is great because healthy disagreements breed healthy organizations. "Having IDPs for everybody is really tough," he says. "That's a difficult investment when the leader's cost per hour is high and you want them to focus on other things that will make money or launch new initiatives. It is logistically hard for leaders who have a lot of direct reports to help build IDPs. IDPs are incredibly important, but they really depend on having somebody with the self-awareness to say, 'I know that I'm not doing something right. I need to figure out how to fix it.'

"When you have those people, they'll have the conversation

with their leader that helps them understand where their gaps are," Eddie goes on. "Then the leader has to have enough self-awareness to give them the type of candid feedback they need. As much as leaders manage down, we have to train employees have to manage up. They need the courage and resolve to have hard conversations with their managers about why they feel like they're not excelling in their roles. Everybody fails at some point, right? It's how you deal with that failure and how you move on from it that determines how successful you are."

Let me highlight two things Eddie said that are especially important:

. . . .

As much as leaders manage down, we have to train employees have to manage up. Everybody fails at some point. It's how you deal with that failure and how you move on from it that determines how successful you are.

. . . .

The Realistic Future of Working from Home

Of course, by the time you're reading this, the issue of how to hire, train, and develop employees in a WFH environment will be clearer. We're already looking at WFH with more healthy skepticism. By the fall of 2020, cracks were appearing in the sunshine-and-roses predictions of a brave new world of completely remote work. As the bloom came off the WFH rose, the press was all over it. The hit podcast *Hidden Brain* ran an episode that featured a Stanford professor's kids interrupting his videoconferences with bagpipe practice, and the host and guests revealed that working from home—and doing it well—is a lot harder and less satisfying that it seemed before the pandemic.

On *ZDNet*, Microsoft CEO Satya Nadella claimed that working from home "lulls you into a stupor."[1] *The Atlantic* ran a piece[2] about how working from home costs young professionals opportunities to socialize, network, and make friends, and they lose out on advancement opportunities because they're not in the office to be noticed. The website *Ladders* reported that "work from home fatigue" seemed to be setting in around the time the kids were scheduled to go back to school but didn't.

The story cited an IBM Institute for Business Value study[3] that found that in August of 2020, 67 percent of American workers said they'd like to continue working from home at least occasionally, down from more than 80 percent mark in July. The same study found that while 65 percent of respondents said in July 2020 that they wanted to work from home permanently, that number was down to 50 percent by August. I could go on (and on and on), but there's no need. By late 2020, the WFH honeymoon had turned into a loveless marriage.

I don't think that's a bad thing. As with any business phenomenon, remote work should be viewed realistically, not with cynicism or through rose-colored glasses. WFH may not be the panacea some believed it would be, but it's not going away either. As with many things in business, the answer to the future of WFH will be "It depends."

Consider that *2020 State of Remote Work* study I cited earlier in this book. In it, 98 percent of respondents said they would like to continue WFH in some capacity for the rest of their careers. Plenty of other surveys and anecdotal reports support the idea that while 100 percent WFH probably won't exist, it will still be around in some form. Large portions of the workforce take to it like ducks to water, and your and every other organization will almost certainly need to find way to accommodate both in-office and remote workforces. In the future, even when organizations are not forced into WFH situations by external events, they will self-sort into two main types:

1. **WFH Native.** These are enterprises founded from the outset as remote companies, companies like Zapier, GitHub, Toptal, Upworthy, and DesignLab. WFH-native orgs are often in tech-centric sectors like coding and app development or information/content fields like writing, design, and video, which makes delivery of products location independent.

   For WFH natives, remote work is baked into their cultures from the beginning. It's part of the business plan, enabling them to hire people who relish working anywhere and are emotionally suited to being self-directed and to promote leaders who are just as comfortable with running a distributed org. For companies like these, reflective leadership, peer learning, and coaching will probably be part of their operating system from day one. These companies will have learned from the lessons of 2020 that making WFH work means upending decades of management tradition, and they'll be fine with that.

   They will also benefit from a global hiring pool. That not only reduces startup costs but drastically levels up any young company's ability to land game-changing talent. DesignLab, which teaches students how to design online user interfaces and develop the user experience, has more than four hundred mentors all over the world and a fully distributed workforce. Zapier, which lets users automate app-based tasks, has three hundred remote employees scattered across seventeen time zones in twenty-eight countries. This will be the new normal. These companies will compete fiercely because of their talent and low overhead.

Because these tech-centric natives will lean heavily toward a global workforce, their cultures will be agile and totally digital, centered on the wonders of avoiding nasty commutes, living anywhere, and maintaining a better work/life balance. Challenges will include maintaining a consistent culture, recruiting people who can thrive in a self-motivated, distributed world and putting in place the kinds of regular touches and warm, authentic cultural fabric that's worked so well for us at JumpCrew.

2. **Hybrid.** These will be everybody else. They will be the corporations like Facebook and Twitter that have announced they plan to allow their people to work remotely "forever" but who will inevitably have a cohort of employees who either want to be or need to be working onsite. It will almost certainly be JumpCrew.

By and large, hybrids will operate with a blend of in-office personnel and people working remotely, employees whose positions afford them the freedom to choose WFH (some, like nurses or law enforcement officers, obviously can't do this). As a result, these organizations will be built around complicated calendars where some employees do all their work from the office, others do all their work from home, and some people work from the office three days and week and at home two days or follow a "one week on, one week off" schedule. Just thinking about it makes my head hurt.

Other hybrids will return to the office as flexible office-remote companies, but as they grow, they will focus on building their workforce primarily by hiring people who can work from home, probably from all over the world.

This has been the JumpCrew model. In the summer of 2020, just as the novelty of WFH was wearing off for some of our people and they were itching to come back to the office and see the colleagues who they missed, we started expanding recruitment beyond Nashville. We began interviewing people from all over not only the U.S. but from all over the planet.

By the fall, I had started having Google Meets with new hires who were from six, eight, even ten different locations. In the future, it's very likely that our company will be a hybrid made of a people who thrive as part of a close-knit F2F tribe of people who work in Nashville, new hires from 2020 and beyond who have always been remote and on occasion come to Nashville for training or events, and executives and managers whose collaboration on strategy and tactics benefit from being predominantly in the hive.

For hybrids, the greatest challenge will be avoiding the "two cultures trap," where there's one set of rules and cultural standards for in-person employees, and another for remote employees. That's a surefire recipe for resentment and conflict, so leaders will need to be mindful and intentional about measures that help everyone in the org feel seen, heard, respected, and cared for.

WFH Changes the Meaning of "Fit"

Worry about the short-term economic environment related to COVID-19 was our catalyst for running a more fiscally disciplined business. What had been a relatively slow process of recognizing people unlikely to excel and exiting them from the organization became a high-speed process out of necessity. In the past, the more relaxed pace of a face-to-face office had given us time to suss out people who could not adapt to the demands of our organization, but WFH concentrated everything. We had to figure out who was most likely to excel *now*.

Why the urgency? Many of our smaller clients struggled. As sales cycles stretched, they struggled to manage their cash flow, and their payments to us slowed or stopped. As the cushion of cash we had raised from investors shrank, we rallied the troops. Fortunately, we already had a strong, tight tribe within JumpCrew—a large and dedicated core that had bonded around a strong sense of community. Instinctively, we knew that community might give us a big edge over competitors who had no idea how to make WFH work. The push forced us to be more deliberate in our hiring, and doing so improved the fabric of the company. We came to think of hiring as a process of building a matrix of relationships.

We did something right, I guess. In 2020, even as so many organizations our size were flailing around trying to get their people settled, we went from EBITDA-negative to EBITDA-positive and built JumpCrew around a core of the most engaged and highest-performing employees. But how did we do that?

One of the things we understood right away was that the radical shift to work from home immediately changed how we had to think about the concept of "fit." In the traditional workplace, a new hire who fits with the established culture is generally someone who shares and appreciates the values, personalities, and norms of the company. They're people who get the prevailing sense of humor, share the mission, and can make your goals their goals without missing a beat. That's still true in the WFH world . . . to a degree. But that's not the whole picture.

Eddie Moncayo also highlights a critical point: *training* is essential to succeed in hiring and developing personnel in WFH. "We'll be doing culture work next year that should help leaders bridge what has become a real divide in how they lead people who are only represented to them in a two-dimensional way," he says. "It's difficult for employees who have always performed in an in-person format to suddenly have the world change and force them to WFH with no runway, time to adjust, or competence to pivot to a virtual environment, and it's equally difficult for many leaders to perform effectively if untrained on how to create, nurture, and maintain virtual relationships with people that in some cases, they will never get to meet in person. It should be underscored how much of a challenge that has become for organizations around the world."

In remote work, fit also comes from seemingly mundane factors, like being able to be meaningfully present over a video chat. It comes from being utterly reliable, so your peers know they can depend on you even when they can't see you working. It comes from knowing that in order for people to feel that you empathize with them, you have to over-communicate and be forceful with your emotions, like a stage actor speaking 20 percent louder than in real life so the audience in the last five rows of the theater can hear you. When we saw that we would have to look for different people with different gifts, we changed our approach for hiring.

We also became much more ruthless about letting people go, as Lavall Chichester, our brilliant former CMO, says. "I had to let someone go who we just weren't on the same page with anymore," he relates. "That was rough, because he was very good at pretending to do work, and he was super talented, but you just no longer wanted him to be on the team. After coaching him and trying to help him figure out what was going on, we realized that we weren't on the same page and he wasn't hitting any of our values. When that happens, we've learned that we just have to let them go."

Look for the "Self-Selectors"

But our key revelation was understanding that everyone working at JumpCrew in 2020 had been forced into working from home. Under normal circumstances, that wouldn't be the case. Employees and prospective hires would sort themselves into the three groups I mentioned: people who want to work from home all the time, people who want to be in the office all the time, and the ones who want a little of both. That wasn't happening in the depths of COVID-19, but we could still keep our eyes out for the self-selectors!

The piece I quoted in *The Atlantic* a few pages ago nails it: "There are tons of studies on the positive benefits of teleworking, but most of that research is interviews and surveys with people who have self-selected into remote work," says Kati Peditto, an environmental design psychologist at the United States Air Force Academy. Workers who value day-to-day flexibility in their schedules are ideal work-from-home candidates; those who like strict boundaries between their professional and personal lives, not so much. Career positioning also matters—people who have already built strong social and professional networks may not suffer much from the lack of face-to-face contact at the office, but for those still trying to make such ties, remote work can be alienating.[4]

In other words, we didn't have to hire people who we could teach to gel in our connected, hyper-reflective, heart-on-the-sleeve WFH culture. We just had to watch for recruits who were already wired to thrive in that environment. Joel Gascoigne and the team at Buffer have found that people with these traits often come from freelance, contracting, or startup backgrounds. They tend to be independent thinkers, flexible, and accustomed to working in nontraditional settings. However, this has not been my experience. Freelancers and people with lots of startups on their CVs want to do things their way and are thus less likely to commit to our way and culture. That's fine, but those aren't the folks most likely to succeed in a connected, "we're all in this together" type of culture.

Task automation software company Zapier has some ideas[5] I agree with about the qualities we should be looking for in a potential A-level remote employee:

An action orientation. Self-starters who will take the initiative and get work done without waiting to be asked.

The ability to prioritize. Someone who knows how to allocate their time and where and when to spend it depending on the goal.

Proficient writing. This one is smart. In WFH, a lot of communication will take place in writing—Slack channels, instant messages, text chats during videoconferences. New hires should have strong "lexical empathy." In other words, they should know how to email and text without being jerks.

Support system. The person you hire should interact with human beings other than the fine folks on the other end of the video chat.

Technical savvy. You'd think this would be obvious, but not everyone can manage their Wi-Fi connection or knows how to use Zoom.

That, however, is the tip of the iceberg if you're looking to build a WFH organization around reflective leadership, coaching, and peer learning. You need a more precise portfolio of traits to find real fit. This is a very new area, so we're learning as we go, but these are some of the other areas we've watched closely in our recruiting:

Psychological Factors. Introverts and extroverts process remote work quite differently and not always as you would expect. Introverts, who can find the constant banter and pressure to socialize mentally exhausting, often thrive in WFH because they can bottleneck the stream of communication until it's just the right size for their comfort. True, you want people who will step out of their comfort zone, but that doesn't happen right away. Over time, introverts can become more extroverted.

> Extroverts, as we've discussed in our talk about salespeople, typically have more trouble working from home. There's no energy source for them to feed on. Still, people are not profiles. Consider these traits to be at the top of your list:

- Organized
- Focused
- Self-disciplined
- Reliable
- Adaptable

- Strong communicator
- Good listener
- Self-aware
- Humble

Experience. Values, communication and collaboration skill, emotional intelligence, drive, the ability to build relationships...in most cases, they matter more than specific job experience in the WFH world. You're hiring people, not resumes. At JumpCrew, we were hiring personal trainers, musicians, waitresses, even a Domino's delivery guy. Some knew little about sales, but they had the character, and they had the hunger to achieve.

Home Environment. This should be obvious. Your recruits should have a physical space conducive not only to work but to a professional appearance and performance. It should be an office, not one corner of a loud kitchen filled with kids and barking dogs. I realize that's not always possible because of where people live or economic factors, so if you really want someone on your team who doesn't have a presentable space, consider renting them an office at a local co-working space . . . or not hiring them.

The Three Pillars. They are central to the extraordinary success we've enjoyed, so why not look for people who have an affinity for these methods? Even if you don't fully adopt my philosophy, any company will benefit from hiring people who are reflective, can coach others, and are open to learning from and teaching colleagues.

Your job as the leader is to try and connect with people in interviews, during onboarding, and after onboarding. That's how you'll start to see if someone is a true fit for your culture and your WFH strategy. If they are, you're home free. If they're not, you have a decision to make. Can you accept where they are today and coach and train them to be more in alignment with your culture down the road? Or should you save your breath and ask them to move on?

Again, the answer is "It depends." Is the new hire productive enough to warrant investment? Are they open-minded and receptive to the idea that the way they approach work could be counterproductive and interfering with their ability to succeed? If you find someone to be eminently coachable, invest the time. However, most new hires can't be coached into fitting into a Three Pillars culture if they aren't ready when they start. That's simply not who they are, and you do them and your organization a favor in letting them go sooner rather than later.

Practical Challenges in Hiring for WFH

Have you tried onboarding new hires via Google Meet during a pandemic? It's strange. But at JumpCrew we've tried to turn the strangeness of the distanced environment to our advantage. Peers often handle onboarding of new employees in keeping with the basic principles of peer learning. These sessions are set up like Circles and are intentionally personal, friendly, and open to anyone questioning anything. They're completely in line with JumpCrew's values.

Onboarding is one of many practical considerations WFH organizations must account for when recruiting from a WFH labor pool. Interviews are another. In neither case will you meet in person with your prospective employees, so it's vital to be prepared with a warm-up process (to evaluate the person's ability to connect) and some good follow-up questions. When I'm interviewing someone without them being present in the room, an entire channel of data about them is closed to me: body language, posture, attire, nervous tics, eye contact, and so on. So I have to ask more direct questions about values and character. What does this person care about? What do they stand for? How do they problem solve? What makes them uncomfortable?

As for answers, I'm looking for trustworthiness above all in a WFH employee. This person will be representing me without anyone else present to keep an eye on them. Are you confident that they will represent you well? Beyond that, I expect JumpCrew candidates to level with me about their opinions and their weaknesses. Be direct, be brave, be clear. WFH demands employees who can speak honestly, mean what they say, and meet high standards for candor and kindness.

WFH is also a unique environment for misunderstandings. Working via video conference creates all sorts of possible scenarios that keep corporate lawyers up at night, from sexual harassment claims because someone told a bad joke to the horror of someone inadvertently coming into the room in a state of undress (just Google now-former *New Yorker* writer Jeffrey Toobin). Success often depends on a group's ability to self-police acceptable behavior. WFH requires a whole new set of HR and legal strategies that are still being formulated. In the meantime, be patient, understanding, and have a sense of humor.

Terminating people takes on a new dimension in WFH too. The needs to the business may change and necessitate change or the individual's skills or performance may not evolve with the changing needs in the business or the individual may not reflect the character and values that it takes to succeed in your community. It's important to cut people loose before they impair your ability to succeed or your culture, like a baseball manager who has the unique instinct to take the ball from his tired pitcher's hand *before* the pitcher can give up the grand slam, not after. For example, while I was writing this book, we parted with a number of executives as part of a restructure. Some exited based on performance; others left because we eliminated their positions. We were direct and clear about our reasons, all the executives received similar levels of communication, and we expected the results would be an amicable with all of them. We've had a lot of success with this type of "parting of the ways" in the past, which is why we have some executives on their second stint with JumpCrew.

It's critical to set expectations early on, especially if your culture is as demanding as ours. We insist on high performance, even from home. We're upfront about what recruits should expect and what we expect of them, so when a termination does occur, it should not be and is rarely a surprise.

However, we're not perfect. In the situation above, one well-liked executive hadn't heard the communications the same way the others did, and his termination came as a shock. The executive ended up angry, breached employment covenants, and jeopardized relationships. Needless to say, the risk of such misunderstandings rises in a WFH organization. To avoid potential disasters, I recommend a multipart WFH termination process:

1. Decide what your criteria are for A, B, and C players in your WFH organization. They might be all about performance and KPIs, or they might be about the ability to adapt to working remotely. Just know what sets off alarm bells.

2. Once the bells go off, decide quickly if the patient can be saved. Is she coachable? Can she admit mistakes and grow, or is she set in her thinking?

3. If the employee can't get to or get back to a measurably positive ROI in a reasonable time frame, then have an honest, empathetic and clear conversation and move on.

Circumstances are always changing, and what may have worked in the past may not in the new reality you are managing. Be clear and be decisive.

Finally, there's the issue of burnout. In September of 2020, *Forbes* reported that 69 percent of WFH workers reported experiencing burnout symptoms.[6] We've talked about some of the likely reasons for this: the feeling that the workday never ends because you're always in the same space, the pressure to perform on Zoom calls, the lack of a social outlet for anxiety or frustration, or just longer hours.

Our kind of organization, by its nature, pushes individuals into a zone of discomfort and frequently a bit beyond. This is even more true in WFH. As the leader, it falls to you to keep your finger on the pulse of your people's work-life balance and to help them achieve it in a way that works for everyone. But this goes beyond the leader. The entire tribe should be encouraged to engage in a healthy self-care regimen, including self-reflection but also eating a healthy diet, exercising, and getting enough sleep. This is one way the community of peers can and should look out for each other.

The Benefits of Hiring for WFH

Of course, things aren't all bleak when it comes to hiring in a WFH world. There are many upsides that we experienced at JumpCrew. The most obvious would be that if people can work from home, your recruiting pool jumps from nearby cities to distant states or, perhaps, the entire planet.

WFH can also be good for retention. Obviously, you're more likely to keep good employees if you hire people who are psychologically and emotionally suited for WFH. Plus, people who might otherwise leave because of work-life balance issues or the need to care for small children can be compelled to stay if offered a good remote work situation. But WFH in and of itself isn't a solution. You have to be proactive about building connections between your new hires and the community, and do it early. According to the O.C. Tanner Institute's 2021 *Global Culture Report*, 20 percent of turnover happens in the first forty-five days of employment.[7] Strong onboarding and paying close attention to any early issues that show up can prevent good people from jumping ship.

Is it possible to build a completely WFH organization with a deep, authentic culture without starting with an organization where workers are face-to-face in an office? It is, but it's difficult. You have to hire with tremendous care, calibrate your culture and the personalities of your recruits with extraordinary precision, operate with a scalpel, and move with great speed. You must apply resources, effort, and relentless repetition to building culture, building community, and building relationships. This will be easier for small organizations, but it's also more complicated if you're in rapid growth mode, as culture becomes both more watered down and more complex the larger your company gets.

The best solution will probably turn out to be the hybrid model, starting with a blend of in-person and WFH personnel (when you're not dealing with a global pandemic, of course). Create an atmosphere where face-to-face work occurs and where remote workers can come in whenever they like to bond with their colleagues and collaborate on projects—or just when they get bored. That's the best of all possible worlds: your WFH employees maintain their independence but have the option to get face time when they need it, you still lower your overhead, and everyone benefits from the unparalleled community-building power of being live in a room together.

There are unquestionably challenges in hiring for WFH. Doing so calls for a great deal more care than simply hiring for the office. But if you use reflective leadership, coaching culture, and peer learning as screening tools to identify folks who are likely to blossom in your WFH community, you boost your chances of building something extraordinary, lasting, and transformative.

Chapter Ten

CAN WFH LOWER THE COST OF LEADING?

As I alluded to in Chapter Nine, by late 2020, the honeymoon phase of WFH was definitely over. Nicholas Bloom, a Stanford University economics professor, studied the effects of WFH on companies and individuals and called it a "productivity disaster" and "ticking time bomb for inequality." Those were big statements to make while most of the professional world was still celebrating the freedom to show up for work in sweatpants and shorts.

In his extensive research, Bloom found that productivity and innovation suffered during the pandemic-driven WFH boom largely due to four major factors that will sound familiar to many remote workers. First, children intrude on work time, often with hilarious and embarrassing results. Second, workers were forced to transition to working from their homes, so they had little time to prepare an appropriate work space, and some simply didn't have spare space in small homes and apartments. Privacy was a huge issue in that it became difficult to find privacy to get work done, but also in the fact that work was now invading the privacy of home.

Finally, people were not able to choose to work from home, and as I highlighted in the previous chapter, choice is a vital factor in determining someone's success or failure in WFH. Given these factors, Bloom predicted that a lack of in-person brainstorming would lead to a falloff in innovation, and that the mental health issues stemming from months of isolation and anxiety would further crush productivity. He also pointed the finger at the "digital divide," citing studies showing that only 65 percent of Americans had fast enough Internet to work remotely. This, he predicted, would further economic inequality as higher-earning information and creative professionals would be able to work at home and advance in their careers while lower-paid and blue-collar workers—particularly people of color—would not.[1]

So much for WFH being a cure-all for business, right? Things are never that simple or black-and-white. However, I have identified one area where I think the WFH revolution—and the Three Pillars that make true WFH community and connection possible—could truly change the world. It just might reduce the toll that business success takes on achievement-based leaders.

Do Leaders Have to Be Michael Jordan?

Earlier, I referenced the ESPN docuseries *The Last Dance*, about Michael Jordan's farewell season with the Chicago Bulls, during which he basically willed his "supporting cast" to a final NBA championship. What has always stood out to me about that 1997–98 season was not simply the greatness of Jordan or the performance of his teammates. It was the incredible personal cost to Jordan of winning one last ring: monomania, alienation, stress, doubt, and damage to his family life and relationships for starters. The price of a championship proved to be incredibly high—too high, in my opinion.

But that price also rings familiar because it sounds like the price I've paid—and watched many other entrepreneurs and corporate leaders pay for the success of their companies. It's the primary reason I encourage entrepreneurially-minded people to take their talents to great companies that will nurture their success and be mindful of their health than to try to walk the path of the self-directed, obsessive entrepreneur. Been there, done that.

Still, many can't resist the siren song of the startup. The all-too-common story begins with a driven, intelligent, visionary man or woman with a hunger to build something and leave a mark on the world. She pursues her idea, finds funding, and builds a startup. But conventional wisdom in the world of business tells her there are only two kinds of entrepreneurs: the quick and the dead. Personal time, family, health—they are all sacrifices on the altar of success. After she's built a unicorn, her peers tell her, she can make it up to her family with a summer in Tuscany.

Maybe she's seen too much Tony Robbins or read too many Tim Ferriss books touting the four-hour work week, but whatever the reason, she decides that she'll go all in, work twenty-hour days, and bring her vision to fruition through sheer will. And to some degree, she does; her company finds some success and scales, builds a customer base, and reaches sustainability. But the personal cost is high: stress-related health problems, compromised nights and weekends that become a source of tension in her relationships, alienation from her children, and a disturbing reckoning with her own ego and need to be liked by everyone. Still, she persists, and in a few years, she becomes one of the few lucky ones, sells the company, and makes millions.

Trouble is, by the time she makes this high-dollar exit, still only forty-five years old, she's fried. Her kids barely recognize her. Maybe she's divorced, burnt out mentally and emotionally. And that's with a successful company! Imagine paying that kind of personal price only to build something that fails, which most startups do. Meanwhile, your peers are joining great organizations and growing in their jobs without the hubris of thinking they have to be the top dog.

Then . . . repeat. The reason there are so many "serial entrepreneurs" roaming around is that the journey effectively breaks you for doing anything else. The farther you go down the path of the entrepreneur, the fewer employment options you have. Who's going to hire a fifty-year-old multi-time startup founder who's spent the last twenty years following their own vision and always being the CEO? At some point, your options narrow to the vanishing point.

That's the Cult of the CEO, and we've accepted that this is the price of being an entrepreneur. But does it have to be? My experiences with building JumpCrew's WFH culture have left me more convinced than ever that there's an alternative. To the clear, the events of the past few years are *giving* us an alternative.

Commitment and depth matter. Rob and I were able to move JumpCrew to WFH quickly and with minimal friction because we had a significant number of employees who treated the business like they owned it. Leaders don't make it on charisma and vision alone. Success relies on the contributions, feedback, and skills of a large group of people. The larger the group, the more unlikely it is you can get them to the promised land through sheer force of will. The trouble is, too many leaders try.

What if the Three Pillars and WFH culture are showing us another way? What if, instead of endless workdays and burnout and a personal life left in cinders, leaders could coach their people and help them develop self-reflection so they could lead *themselves* to the next level, and even surpass the coach? What if the price of leading didn't have to be so damned high?

No More Strongman

After my second successful exit in 2015, I ended up in Barcelona, scorched and exhausted. I had known better, yet circumstances played into my need and desire to be my failing company's savior—and we know how history has treated saviors. After sinking the last of my available cash into my company when the investors refused, I escaped with a win on paper. But I ended up sacrificing what was left of my own well-being. The demands of running a business and being a single dad had taken a toll on me. My program of being the good boy who puts others first had long since outlived its usefulness, and I finally saw that. I stopped seeing self-care as selfish.

Barcelona turned out to be a life-altering experience for the better. I fell in with a group of mindful, reflective ex-pat entrepreneurs, leaders who helped me turn my perceptions inward. But I don't think hitting bottom should be a standard part of the leadership rite of passage.

Jerry Colonna agrees. When I asked him about the idea that perhaps the cost of leadership need not be so high in this new world, he responded, "The way I would unpack this question is, what are our definitions of success? We presume a universal agreement around the definition of success, just like we presume universal agreement around the definition of wealth."

Jerry also talks about the idea of the "strongman," which is common in politics but also applies to the alpha-dog business ethos. The strongman myth says that true leaders are authoritarians who reject negotiation and diplomacy in favor of using force to work their will. In the end, being a strongman is all about the leader's ego, which means that everyone else is expendable. While you might be able to govern a nation that way (temporarily), that's no way to grow an organization. If you're a demagogue, people will simply quit.

It's relatively easy to hang our success on indicators that don't value personal growth and don't cost us much in terms of facing fear or acknowledging our emotions. Instead, we often hang success on bank account balances, a house, and a car. That's a lot less frightening than looking at what's holding us back and triggers our defensive, elusive behaviors that produce negative outcomes. It's safer and easier to say, "Well, I can't sleep at night and my kids hate me, but check out all this cool shit that I own." True success means becoming aware of who you are and how your actions and programs are holding you back.

"It's about answers to questions," Jerry continues. "What kind of leader would you like to be? What kind of adult would you like to be? What kind of company would you like to build or work for? As I say in my book, if your child were to come to work for your company, how would you feel? *Every* one of your employees is somebody's parent, somebody's child, or somebody's sibling. I am not afraid to stop people and say, 'Stop, look at your life.' How would you want someone to treat your daughter? How would you want them to speak with her? That's how you should engage, right to the heart."

The WFH environment and the Three Pillars work synergistically to give leaders hooked on the myth of the traditional leader a chance to go in a different direction. Because leaders are no longer the kings of the office suite and can't lead by their mere presence, WFH necessitates leading with self-reflection and mindfulness, coaching instead of ordering, being present for the entire video meeting, and giving individual contributors the space, safety, and trust to teach one another. The new rules insist that you slow down; look within; ask for commitments, connection, and trust; and demonstrate mutual respect.

By asking the emerging leaders on your team to help you build your remote culture, you're asking your people to lead alongside you by representing the values that guide your organization. So long Machiavelli, hello Brené Brown.

In my first sales training, I learned about this as the "Columbo Principle," named after the old detective TV series starring Peter Falk. If you ask for help, people are inclined to give it. In sales talk, we call this "the upfront verbal contract." The leader embodies this truth by being the first one to ask for help and be humble, the first to get his or her hands dirty, the first to admit they screwed something up, the first to risk looking silly, and the first to share and be vulnerable. Leading stops being about being about giving the answer and starts being about asking better questions.

The Blessings of Being a Leader

My goal is to reboot leadership and entrepreneurship in a way so that we can begin enjoying the real blessings that it can bring to everyone. And done right, it can be a tremendously creative, enriching experience. Adam Stettner, CEO of small business finance company Reliant Funding, expressed this perfectly in an interview with *Authority* magazine:

> Leading is all consuming, especially when you do it with passion. It costs time and creates the need for sacrifice in all areas of your life. That places stress on everything and can create doubt. Doubt in your approach or in your ability. This is true regardless of how ready you think you are. This self-doubt is healthy, provided it doesn't consume you...This business process then cycles into your personal life and helps you to strengthen your time, life and relationship management skills. Leading at this level breaks you down and then builds you back up stronger than before.[2]

Leading and growing a business, building a community, connecting with and inspiring people, and creating ideas that can change the world and make people's lives better—these experiences should change *leaders* for the better as well. The fact that they often do the opposite doesn't mean there's something wrong with the concept of founding an organization, building a tribe of like-minded people, and growing it to its full potential. It means we've let our baggage containing our negative emotions, our unacknowledged pain, loss, resentment and fear get in the way of doing it *right*. It's time for that to change.

The Darwinian instinct, the teaching of Machiavellian behavior, and the idolatry of *The Art of War* by generations of leaders has created a myth of how a "real" leader leads that has obstructed our ability to evolve. Replacing that thinking with the precepts of reflection, self-awareness, and teaching enables leaders to forge an organization of like-minded individuals who aspire to function as a group, put the community first, and care for themselves and each other on the same level of importance as the bottom line. That enterprise fills us up personally as well as professionally.

This new model is not only humanistic but also promotes healing. The relationships, challenges, and demands of growing a business become the crucible in which leaders are able to hold themselves accountable, embrace change, accept their limitations, and grow. From that perspective, leading stops being about filling emptiness and starts being about moving past it to something better.

It's time we accepted that building a company and a team isn't about fixing what's broken in our lives or anyone else's. It's certainly not about papering over pain with power games or false celebrity. It's also not the job of the people you hire, who have placed so much faith in you, to validate you or absolve you from whatever you've done wrong. *You* owe *them* your commitment to doing your work, not the other way around. Leading is an honor; it has little to do with title. It is a standing you earn by doing. If coming to an understanding of reflective leadership, coaching, and peer learning has taught me anything, it's that I have to find the best way to meet my own needs and be deferential to the needs of the team. Whenever possible, the needs of the team come first, and when I put them first, my needs are ultimately met, too, in more ways than I ever anticipated.

Leaders who come to that understanding:

- Master group dynamics;
- Develop deeper, more satisfying relationships with everyone in the org;
- Communicate in an accurate and timely way;
- Relish working in a collaborative environment; and
- Embrace continuous learning outside their comfort zone.

Being an entrepreneur and a leader should lift you up, not burn you out. It should not make you feel your choices are binary: get your dream job or start your dream company and give up everything else in your life versus keep your time, health, and family and spend your life wondering "What if?" That's a false choice. If you launch a business or step up to big new role, you accept some risk, and your quality of life may take a brief hit until you adjust. If you can't, it's on you to communicate that clearly.

For almost twenty years, I worked with a wonderful woman who could not say no to any project. We jokingly called her "the sweeper" as she swept endless data, projects, and deliverables under the rug because, inevitably, she took on more than she could handle. She was lovable and trustworthy but uncoachable. We accepted her limitations as they were more than offset by the trust she earned. However, if I worked with her today, I would be asking how we could change her role so it was more sustainable. That should be the rule for all leaders. Let's be done with this idea that success means a scorched-earth personal life and draining away your last drop of serotonin, okay? It's obsolete, and it was never necessary. We can do better.

How the Pillars and WFH Change the Game

In fact, the mass move to WFH has already changed the game substantively by letting our affinity for in-person outbursts die in a vacuum of shared physical space. Corporate leaders have suddenly found themselves evicted from the C-suite, and that has created a kind of new freedom to reinvent what it means to lead. Suddenly, we're holding morning meetings on Zoom in lounge pants and pandemic beards. Everything is more casual, heated exchanges have less heat, and contentious discussions are a bit more jocular.

These circumstances have also forced us to find new ways to coach, mentor, instruct, teach, and discipline our people. Because we couldn't do it directly, leading had to come more through influence, affection, community, technology, and a sense of duty and responsibility suffused throughout entire organizations. That brings us full circle back to the Three Pillars, which are, after all, tools for nurturing things like affection and community within a disparate collection of individuals. Leadership changed, and in having to adapt, we figured out that we didn't necessarily have to go back to the punishing way things had been.

The Pillars and the WFH environment change the equation for leaders. They allow for greater entrepreneurial success inside the safety of an already successful organization because of the following reasons:

Emerging leaders have equal opportunity to inspire, motivate, and accelerate achievement. We experienced this on numerous occasions in the past year, none as impactful as our all-hands meeting addressing the Black Lives Matter protests. The directives of coaching culture are "ask, listen, share, and don't tell." When it goes well, there is a feedback loop between it, peer learning, and reflective leadership and then your team stops looking at you for all the answers. The challenge (until you can't afford to accept it any longer) is to encourage teammates to find and use new tools, widen their lens, and discover knowledge for themselves.

Posturing and preening are dead. The new world values authenticity, not attitude. Leaders can be themselves, not some character from an HBO series.

You're allowed to be real, flawed, and struggling. The idea that weakness and human failings are for losers has poisoned generations of leaders into believing they had to project a perfect superman (or woman) image. But one of the quickest ways to connect meaningfully and honestly is to admit you were wrong or that you don't know the answer. Get past the force field of authority that so many new executives struggle with and reach your people.

> For example, I think the hardest job at JumpCrew is Team Lead. Our Team Leads not only still carry a sales quota but also have to navigate the dynamic change of going from being a peer to managing them. The ones who fail are often the ones who fall victim to the traditional boss stereotype fail and lose their friends—and eventually their jobs too. Instead, be real. Admit your doubts and challenges, and ask for help like Columbo did! Be a person. Your colleagues respect you for it because we all experience doubts, and owning up to them is a sign of wisdom.

You have permission to put human needs first, including yours. In this environment, the entire culture acknowledges that people, not some amorphous company, matter most. So their needs matter too: personal time off, family, children, spiritual fulfillment, grief. Those were often afterthoughts in Business 1.0, barriers to profit and getting things done. Now they're *part* of the community you are in and part of getting things done. The great thing is, your personal needs matter too.

The adrenaline rush of being the go-to person for everything—we're questioning it now. Actually, we're burying it. It's the old program, outdated and slow. But the dominant feature of entrepreneurship and corporate leadership in the past was that it became the beast that ate your time. Unless you could drag yourself out of bed at 4 a.m. to hit the gym, every waking moment was fodder for the success machine.

That's no longer the case. Time is the most obvious resource in WFH. Now, there's more of it. Time to reflect, connect, embrace self-care, and write. You're less accessible, and so you're less interruptible. You can walk the dog in the middle of the day, help the kids with their homework, and be home by five because you never left. You're no longer one of the 4.3 million workers who had commutes of ninety minutes or more in 2018.[3] You're free.

Maybe most critical of all, the pillars and remote leading encourage leaders to build an identity that values more than titles and compensation. Perpetual aspiration is not a recipe for happiness and fulfillment. Generations of leaders have allowed their professional status to define their identities, much to the detriment of their own growth. Journalist Derek Thompson writes about "The Gospel of Work," or what he calls *workism*: "the belief that work is not only necessary to economic production, but also the centerpiece of one's identity and life's purpose; and the belief that any policy to promote human welfare must always encourage more work."[4]

Reflection, openness, and community, along with respect for the needs of the humans who make an organization run, are the antivenom for the toxin of workism. When work helps you discover your value to others as a coach, mentor, teacher, collaborator and a better spouse, parent, and friend, you don't need it to define who you are. You'll know.

The Alternative Entrepreneur

That said, the risk of burnout remains. For one thing, as we have established, working from home can increase the chances of burnout when your workday seems to extend endlessly. Even the most enlightened leader will still need self-discipline, clear boundaries between work and home life, support from family or colleagues, sound self-care, and the chance to step away and reboot from time to time.

Ben Fanning, author of *The Quit Alternative: The Blueprint for Creating the Job You Love Without Quitting*, has become something of a crusader against burnout. In his Burnout Manifesto, he views burnout as an opportunity for change, a red flag from your heart and mind shouting at you, "What you're doing isn't good for you! It's time to do something else!" He preaches an end to passively accepting your fate and making work personal, both of which I agree with.[5]

Burnout can be a life-changing wakeup call . . . if you choose to see it that way. Most important, burnout isn't destiny. Leading or launching a company doesn't inevitably have to lead to divorce or spending a year living silently in a Trappist monastery. You can prevent burnout by accepting some other truths courtesy of Ben Fanning:

1. You don't have to throw away your current career to have one that's inspired (most are relieved by this).
2. Your path to reigniting your career starts by learning something new.
3. You can have an inspired career, but you have to get around to understanding yourself now (not after the fact).
4. You can do much, much more than you realize.
5. There is almost always a better way.[6]

Let's do a thought experiment. What would the life of an entrepreneur or corporate leader look like if reflective leadership and everything else we've talked about were the norms? If leaders were free to work from home when they wanted and be themselves, and they ignored executive stereotypes, were vulnerable and real, and led with passion and inspiration? How would the leadership story play out? I think it might look something like this:

Chapter 1. The leader starts a company or joins an existing company with the goal of helping it become great. Everything begins with a vision. If you can't see and articulate it, no one will follow you.

Chapter 2. They become an integral part of a team that is building an environment filled with peers who value achievement, growth, self-awareness, and the power of coaching and peer learning. They share the values of the organization from the top down. Our core values were defined by our leadership team. The only thing Rob changed at JumpCrew was putting diversity at the top of our core values. Then infuse your shared values into the organization through coaching culture.

Chapter 3. They infuse the Three Pillars into the organization, and encourage self-reflection, greater bonding, and sharing. A sense of tribal loyalty and trust forms. Team accountability soars as no one individual wants to be the one to let down what has become a second family. You are a coach who will still make executive decisions as needed and maintain both the integrity of the org and its values.

Chapter 4. The struggle is real. The company is growing, work is hard, and hours are long, and yet there is less stress and friction in the organization. The "band of brothers" aura helps keep everyone motivated, and at the same time, everyone is expected to set boundaries for self-care and stay healthy. Conflicts resolve through candor and compassion while the organization gets smarter through peer-to-peer sharing and teaching.

Chapter 5. This is the "Life is Great" stage. You have community, impact, and enthusiastic collaboration. You're optimized for achievement, satisfaction, and financial reward, well-positioned for growth and ready to produce the next generation of reflective leaders who can take the organization to the next level.

That may seem like pie-in-the-sky, but it's really not. Creating a corporate culture, a business culture where the cost of success is not ruinously high is a matter of will rather than a matter of taking action. It has happened in the WFH era because some leaders saw the crisis as an opportunity to disrupt the way business was done. It's possible.

It's possible because we aspire to create more than an organization. We aspire to build a community whose boundaries extend beyond the organization. People can leave the company and stay in the community, be supportive of one another, and carry their goals and shared ambition to other companies. Now that the JumpCrew community extends beyond Nashville, it can impact hundreds of local communities as our members spread our key messages: being the best you can be, discovering your ability to be great and helping others find their greatness, coaching, and actively listening to people who think differently. Our community can help bring people together, even if they're never on the JumpCrew payroll. In such a scenario, what does a leader or founder's exit look like? It certainly wouldn't have to be the desperate flight from psychic and spiritual depletion that I experienced in my last company and saw in so many others. Exiting could become an affirming choice. Leaders would stay in a job as long as it worked for them and for the organization. When the needs and demands of life changed or the needs and demands of the organization changed, they would change.

Opportunities would arise, and company missions, priorities, and roles would transform, and when the time came to move on to something else, maybe something manifestly *not* work, leaders would take the next step in their journey. If that's you, maybe you're lucky enough that your company has grown so big so fast that you are able to sell. Either way, the transition is a time of joy and renewal, made with respect for the relationships and the community the organization helped create.

That may seem far-fetched, but not long ago, the idea that the business world would go virtual practically overnight seemed impossible. Change seems implausible . . . until it happens. Then it seems inevitable. And someone always has to begin it, to see five minutes farther down the road than everyone else. Maybe, for your organization, that's you.

Mr. Spooner, my curmudgeonly high school driver's ed teacher, said to everyone, "Aim high when you're steering, son. If you can't see past what's right in front of you, you'll crash." And so I have tried. I've always lifted my head and looked out farther. I advise you to do the same. Because when you don't aim high, what's probable may or may not happen, but what's possible will only happen when you aim higher.

I want to close with a wonderful insight from therapist and author Esther Perel, expressed on the Sway podcast. In talking about working from home, she drilled down beautifully into the irreplaceability of our relationships with each other:

> Everyone's talking about empathic leadership, the soft skills gap, the importance of wellness and mental health in the workplace. Everyone understands that certain things can remain remote and maybe there's an advantage to that. And if there is an option for hybrid, that's OK...We can accomplish things. It's not like we can't. But task is only one portion of what happens at work. And, especially today, work is an identity project. It's a place where we go to experience meaning, community, belonging, purpose. And money, and survival.[7]

Perfectly said. We need each other, perhaps now more than ever. We need each other's wisdom, heart, and humanity, even if we can only be together for now via a Zoom call or a Slack channel. We need the tribe, the family. The wise leaders of the future will be the ones who understand that and work to make it happen.

ACKNOWLEDGMENTS

Many people have contributed to my successes and this book. Naren Aryal and Kristin Perry believed this book would make a difference, and Tim Vandehey, my editing sage, made this story readable.

Much of this book is about JumpCrew. I'd like to thank not just those who sat for interviews and are quoted within, but to all of those who invested any part of their careers in the company's growth. And a special thank you to my cofounder and JumpCrew CEO, Robert Henderson, and Jerry Colonna, whose book *Reboot: Leadership and the Art of Growing Up* inspired me to dig deeper and into the fabric of what connects all of us. Thank you for connecting your work and your story to *Remote Leadership*.

I grew up surrounded by entrepreneurs. My parents, Bernard and Vivian, were gritty merchants despite not having college degrees, and my brother, Paul Metselaar, used the power of an optimist and focus to turn a bankrupt travel agency into a $1 billion travel management company.

My friend Elliott Greene gave me Peter Senge's *The Fifth Discipline* thirty years ago, and it would become the foundation of my leadership development and set me on a journey of self-discovery.

Humility and compassion are underappreciated traits of successful entrepreneurs, and they are just a small part of the gifts Arlene Pachter left to me. My first wife pushed me to start a business as she began cancer treatment. She challenged me, set the highest bar for courage, and gave me the biggest most lasting gift, a daughter.

Finally, thank you to Stephanie Jules and everyone who read this book in its early stages and provided their thoughts along the way. As with everything I strive to do, this was a team effort.

ENDNOTES

Introduction

1   "Workers who could work at home, did work at home, and were paid for work at home, by selected characteristics, averages for the period 2017-2018," U.S. Bureau of Labor Statistics, https://www.bls.gov/news.release/flex2.t01.htm, accessed August 20, 2020.

2   Kamouri, Anita, Lister, Kate, Global Work-From-Home Experience Survey, pg. 10, https://globalworkplaceanalytics.com/wp-content/uploads/edd/2020/05/Global-Work-from-Home-Experience-Survey-Report-FINAL.pdf, accessed August 31, 2020.

3   "Reviewing Remote Work in the U.S. Under COVID-19," The Gallup Organization, May 22, 2020, https://news.gallup.com/poll/311375/reviewing-remote-work-covid.aspx, accessed August 22, 2020.

4   Davis, Alexander, "VC poised for another shakeup as workers abandon tech hubs," *PitchBook*, May 26, 2020, https://pitchbook.com/news/articles/vc-poised-for-another-shakeup-as-workers-abandon-tech-hubs, accessed August 24, 2020.

5   "Work in the time of coronavirus," Monster.com, poll results July 10-13, 2020, https://learnmore.monster.com/poll-results-from-work-in-the-time-of-coronavirus, accessed September 1, 2020.

6   Levenson, Alec, McLaughlin, Patrick, "New Leadership Challenges for the Virtual World of Work," *MIT Sloan Management Review*, June 4, 2020, https://sloanreview.mit.edu/article/new-leadership-challenges-for-the-virtual-world-of-work, accessed September 3, 2020.

Chapter One

1   Chua, Amy, Rubenfeld, Jed, "What Drives Success?" *New York Times*, January 25, 2014, https://www.nytimes.com/2014/01/26/opinion/sunday/what-drives-success.html, accessed December 17, 2020.

2   Ramamoorthy, Ajay, "A new way to think about Coercive Leadership," *Upshotly*, July 17, 2019, https://www.upshotly.com/blog/coercive-leadership, accessed Sept. 13, 2020.

3   Cohen, Arianne, "The surprising traits of good remote leaders," *BBC Worklife*, September 9, 2020, https://www.bbc.com/worklife/article/20200827-why-in-person-leaders-may-not-be-the-best-virtual-ones, accessed Sept. 13, 2020

4   CultureX, Josh Bersin, Waggl, "The COVID-19 Pulse of HR Survey," *MIT Sloan Management Review*, June 3, 2020, https://sloanreview.mit.edu/article/five-ways-leaders-can-support-remote-work, accessed September 2, 2020.

5   Courtney, Emily, "27 Companies That Have Switched to Long-Term Remote Work," FlexJobs, September 8, 2020, https://www.flexjobs.com/blog/post/companies-switching-remote-work-long-term, accessed September 14, 2020.

6   Egan, Matt, "The office, as you know it, is dead," *CNN Business*, August 25, 2020, https://www.cnn.com/2020/08/25/business/office-space-remote-work-pandemic/index.html, accessed September 8, 2020.

Chapter Two

1   Logan, D., & King, J. P. (2008). *Tribal Leadership*. New York, NY: Harper Business.

2   Bonchek, Mark, "Why the Problem With Learning Is Unlearning," *Harvard Business Review*, November 3, 2016, https://hbr.org/2016/11/why-the-problem-with-learning-is-unlearning, accessed September 14, 2020.

3   Bloom, Nicholas & Liang, James & Roberts, John & Ying, Zhichun. (2013). "Does Working from Home Work? Evidence from a Chinese Experiment." *The Quarterly Journal of Economics*. 130. 10.1093/qje/qju032.

4   "Latest Work-At-Home/Telecommuting/Mobile Work/Remote Work Statistics," *Global Workplace Analytics*, March 13, 2020, https://globalworkplaceanalytics.com/telecommuting-statistics, accessed September 6, 2020.

5   OWL Labs, "State of Remote Work 2019," September 2019, https://www.owllabs.com/state-of-remote-work/2019, accessed September 18, 2020.

6   Bailenson, Jeremy & Yee, Nick & Blascovich, Jim & Beall, Andrew & Lundblad, Nicole & Jin, Michael. (2008). "The Use of Immersive Virtual Reality in the Learning Sciences: Digital Transformations of Teachers, Students, and Social Context." *Journal of the Learning Sciences*. 17. 102-141. 10.1080/10508400701793141.

7   Newport, Cal, "Why Remote Work Is So Hard—and How It Can Be Fixed," *The New Yorker,* May 26, 2020, https://www.newyorker.com/culture/annals-of-inquiry/can-remote-work-be-fixed, accessed August 4, 2020.

8   Buffer, AngelList, "The 2020 State of Remote Work," https://lp.buffer.com/state-of-remote-work-2020, accessed August 30, 2020.

9   Holt-Lunstad, Julianne, et al. "Loneliness and Social Isolation as Risk Factors for Mortality: A Meta-Analytic Review." *Perspectives on Psychological Science,* vol. 10, no. 2, Mar. 2015, pp. 227–237, doi:10.1177/1745691614568352.

10 Sene, Al "Currents," *Digital Ocean,* July 17, 2019, https://www.digitalocean.com/blog/currents-july2019/, accessed September 13, 2020.

11 Rock, David, "The Science of Virtual Work," *Psychology Today,* April 8, 2020, https://www.psychologytoday.com/us/blog/your-brain-work/202004/the-science-virtual-work, accessed August 27, 2020.

12 Bariso, Justin, "This Company's New 2-Sentence Remote Work Policy Is the Best I've Ever Heard," *Inc.,* July 20, 2020, https://www.inc.com/justin-bariso/this-companys-new-2-sentence-remote-work-policy-is-best-ive-ever-heard.html, accessed August 24, 2020.

13 Bariso, Justin, "This Company's Approach to Remote Work Is the Worst I've Ever Seen," *Inc.,* September 20, 2020, https://www.inc.com/justin-bariso/this-companys-approach-to-remote-work-is-worst-ive-ever-seen-emotional-intelligence.html, accessed August 24, 2020.

Chapter Three

1   Smith TW, Uchino BN, Berg CA, Florsheim P, Pearce G, Hawkins M, Hopkins PN, Yoon HC. "Hostile personality traits and coronary artery calcification in middle-aged and older married couples: different effects for self-reports versus spouse ratings." *Psychosom Med.* 2007 Jun;69(5):441-8. doi: 10.1097/PSY.0b013e3180600a65. PMID: 17585063.

2   Gelles, David, "For Helping Immigrants, Chobani's Founder Draws Threats," *New York Times*, October 31, 2016.

3   Ulukaya, Hamdi, "Chobani founder: Higher wages important to our success," *CNN*, March 31, 2016, https://money.cnn.com/2016/03/31/news/economy/chobani-minimum-wage/index.html, accessed September 28, 2020.

4   Süleyman Davut Göker and Kıvanç Bozkuş (February 1, 2017). "Reflective Leadership: Learning to Manage and Lead Human Organizations," *Contemporary Leadership Challenges*, Aida Alvinius, IntechOpen, DOI: 10.5772/64968. Available from: https://www.intechopen.com/books/contemporary-leadership-challenges/reflective-leadership-learning-to-manage-and-lead-human-organizations.

5   Gunaratana, Henepola, *Mindfulness in Plain English* (Boston: Wisdom Publications), 2011, p. 134.

6   Tolle, E. *The Power of Now: A Guide to Spiritual Enlightenment*. (New York: New World Library) 2004, pg 35.

7   Cohn, Jeffrey, Rangan, U. Srinivasa, "Why CEOs Should Model Vulnerability," *Harvard Business Review*, May 11, 2020, https://hbr.org/2020/05/why-ceos-should-model-vulnerability, accessed September 29, 2020.

Chapter Four

1   Whitehurst, Jim, "Leaders Can Shape Company Culture Through Their Behaviors," *Harvard Business Review*, October 13, 2016, https://hbr.org/2016/10/leaders-can-shape-company-culture-through-their-behaviors, accessed September 26, 2020.

2   Tay SW, Ryan P, Ryan CA. Systems 1 and 2 thinking processes and cognitive reflection testing in medical students. Can Med Educ J. 2016;7(2):e97-e103. Published October 18, 2016.

3   Brown, B., *Dare to Lead: Brave Work. Tough Conversations. Whole Hearts.* (New York: Random House) 2018.

4   Chief Executive, "New Survey Finds CEOs Want to Talk Sales, Not Social Issues, in 2019," *Chief Executive*, January 24, 2019, https://chiefexecutive.net/survey-ceos-sales-social-issues/, accessed September 28, 2020.

Chapter Five

1   Dixon, Matthew and Adamson, Brent, "Selling Is Not About Relationships," *Harvard Business Review*, September 30, 2011, https://hbr.org/2011/09/selling-is-not-about-relatio, accessed June 27, 2020.

2   Goldsmith, Marshall, "You Can't Coach the 'Uncoachables,'" https://www.marshallgoldsmith.com/articles/you-cant-coach-the-uncoachables/, accessed October 1, 2020.

3   Institute for Corporate Productivity, "Creating a Coaching Culture," 2014, file:///Users/TimmyV/Downloads/Creating_a_Coaching_Culture_i4cp2014_Preview.pdf.

4   Filipkowski, Jenna, Heverin, Abby, Ruth, Mark, "Building a Coaching Culture with Managers and Leaders," The International Coach Federation in partnership with the Human Capital Institute, September 21, 2016, https://www.careercompasscanada.com/wp-content/uploads/2016/10/2016-Building-a-Coaching-Culture-for-Managers-and-Leaders-Final.compressed.pdf, accessed July 6, 2020.

5   Wooden, J., *They Call Me Coach* (New York: McGraw-Hill Education) 2003.

6   Griffith, Daniel B., "The Leader's Role in Coaching Employees through Conflict," Higher Ed Jobs, April 18, 2016, https://www.higheredjobs.com/articles/articleDisplay.cfm?ID=882, accessed September 30, 2020.

7   Galagan, Pat, Bingham, Tony, "M'm M'm Good: Learning and Performance at Campbell Soup Company," Association for Talent Development, March 2011, https://www.td.org/magazines/td-magazine/mm-mm-good-learning-and-performance-at-campbell-soup-company, accessed October 4, 2020.

8   The Hudson Institute, "Spot Coaching," https://hudsoninstitute.com/organizations/spot-coaching/, accessed August 27, 2020.

Chapter Six

1   Review, Harvard Business, Goleman, D., Boyatzis, R. E., McKee, A., & Finkelstein, S. "HBR's 10 Must Reads on Emotional Intelligence" (with featured article "What Makes a Leader?" by Daniel Goleman) (HBR's 10 Must Reads) (Cambridge: Harvard Business Review Press) 2015.

2   Berglas, Steven, "The Very Real Dangers of Executive Coaching," *Harvard Business Review,* June 2002, https://hbr.org/2002/06/the-very-real-dangers-of-executive-coaching, accessed October 12, 2020.

3   Senge, P. M., *The Fifth Discipline: The Art & Practice of The Learning Organization* (New York: Doubleday) 2006.

4   Sinek, S., *Start with Why: How Great Leaders Inspire Everyone to Take Action* (New York: Portfolio) 2011.

5   Connors, R., Smith, T., & Hickman, C. *The Oz Principle: Getting Results Through Individual and Organizational Accountability,* pg. 6 (New York: Portfolio) 2010.

Chapter Seven

1   Boutwell, Lauren, "Peer Learning: Why It's So Important for Remote Teams,"
    Brainshark.com, June 16, 2020, https://www.brainshark.com/ideas-blog/2020/
    june/peer-learning-why-its-so-important-remote-teams, accessed October 27,
    2020.

2   Duke, A. *Thinking in Bets: Making Smarter Decisions When You Don't Have All
    the Facts* (Illustrated ed.) (New York: Portfolio) 2019 p. 27.

3   Imperative, 2019 Workforce Purpose Index, 2019, https://www.2019wpi.com/,
    accessed August 17, 2020.

4   Griffiths, S., Houston, K., Lazenbatt, A. and Baume, C., 1995. Enhancing Stu-
    dent Learning Through Peer Tutoring In Higher Education: A Compendium
    Resource Pack. Belfast: University of Ulster.

5   Ashford, S. & George, Elizabeth & Blatt, Ruth. (2007). 2 Old Assumptions,
    New Work: The Opportunities and Challenges of Research on Nonstandard
    Employment. Academy of Management Annals. 1. 65-117. 10.5465/078559807.

6   Duhigg, Charles, "What Google Learned From Its Quest to Build the Per-
    fect Team," *New York Times*, February 25, 2016, https://www.nytimes.
    com/2016/02/28/magazine/what-google-learned-from-its-quest-to-build-
    the-perfect-team.html, accessed September 22, 2020.

7   Kolk, V. B. *The Body Keeps the Score: Brain, Mind, and Body in the Healing of
    Trauma* (Illustrated ed.). (New York: Penguin Books) 2015.

8   Klein, Brandon, "What 'Facilitation' Really Means And Why It's Key To The
    Future Of Work," *Fast Company*, September 2017, https://www.fastcompany.
    com/40467377/what-facilitation-really-means-and-why-its-key-to-the-future-
    of-work, accessed July 30, 2020.

Chapter Eight

1   Milian, Victorio, "Peer-to-Peer Learning Can Help Employees Find Value," ADP Spark, https://www.adp.com/spark/articles/2019/03/peer-to-peer-learning-can-help-employees-find-value.aspx#:~:text=Peer%2Dto%2Dpeer%20learning%20in%20the%20workplace%20can%20be%20used,of%20their%20own%20professional%20development, accessed November 6, 2020.

2   Mercer, "Global Talent Trends 2020," June 2020, https://www.mercer.com/content/dam/mercer/attachments/private/global-talent-trends-2020-report.pdf, accessed October 15, 2020.

3   Golden, Ryan, "How HR can encourage peer-to-peer learning in an era of remote work," HR DIVE, November 10, 2020, https://www.hrdive.com/news/how-hr-can-encourage-peer-to-peer-learning-in-an-era-of-remote-work/588738/, accessed November 14, 2020.

Chapter Nine

1   Matyszczyk, Chris, "Microsoft's CEO is tired of working from home and he's not alone," ZDNet, October 9, 2020, https://www.zdnet.com/article/microsofts-ceo-is-tired-of-working-from-home-and-hes-not-alone/, accessed November 6, 2020.

2   Mull, Amanda, "Generation Work-From-Home May Never Recover," *The Atlantic*, October 2020, https://www.theatlantic.com/magazine/archive/2020/10/career-costs-working-from-home/615472/, accessed November 11, 2020.

3   IBM, "COVID-19 Consumer Survey," September 2019, https://www.ibm.com/thought-leadership/institute-business-value/report/covid-19-consumer-survey, accessed October 28, 2020.

4   Mull, Amanda, "Generation Work-From-Home May Never Recover," *The Atlantic*, October 2020, https://www.theatlantic.com/magazine/archive/2020/10/career-costs-working-from-home/615472/, accessed November 11, 2020.

5   Debrule, Sara, Foster, Wade, "How to hire a remote team," *Zapier*, June 22, 2020, https://zapier.com/learn/remote-work/how-to-hire-remote-team/, accessed September 29, 2020.

6   Stahl, Ashley, "Work From Home Burnout: Causes and Cures," *Forbes*, September 1, 2020, https://www.forbes.com/sites/ashleystahl/2020/09/01/work-from-home-burnout-causes-and-cures/?sh=7961b18db881, accessed October 28, 2020.

7   O.C. Tanner Institute, 2021 Global Culture Report, O.C. Tanner Institute, October 2020, https://www.octanner.com/content/dam/oc-tanner/images/v2/culture-report/2021/GCR-2021-sm.pdf, accessed November 17, 2020.

Chapter Ten

1   Bloom, Nicholas, "Stanford professor on the new remote work economy: A 'productivity disaster' and 'ticking time bomb for inequality,'" CNBC, October 8, 2020, https://www.cnbc.com/amp/2020/10/07/stanford-professor-not-optimistic-about-work-from-home-economy-ticking-time-bomb-for-inequality.html, accessed November 2, 2020.

2   Weiner, Yitzi, "Being a CEO is going to cost you more of everything than you think, but the return is worth it," *Authority*, May 7, 2018, https://medium.com/authority-magazine/being-a-ceo-is-going-to-cost-you-more-of-everything-than-you-think-but-the-return-is-worth-it-1f9d5e286471, accessed November 1, 2020.

3 Ingraham, Christopher, "Nine days on the road. Average commute time reached a new record last year," *The Washington Post*, October 7, 2019, https://www. washingtonpost.com/business/2019/10/07/nine-days-road-average-commute-time-reached-new-record-last-year/, accessed December 5, 2020.

4 Thompson, Derek, "Workism Is Making Americans Miserable," *The Atlantic*, February 24, 2019, https://www.theatlantic.com/ideas/archive/2019/02/religion-workism-making-americans-miserable/583441/, accessed September 17, 2020.

5 Fanning, Ben, "The Burnout Manifesto," May 2012, https://www.benfanning.com/wp-content/uploads/2012/05/Burnout.pdf, accessed October 9, 2020.

6 Fanning, Ben, "The Burnout Specialist," website, https://www.benfanning.com/about-us/, accessed October 9, 2020.

7 Perel, Esther, interview, "Post-Election Therapy with Esther Perel," *Sway* podcast, November 9, 2020, https://www.nytimes.com/2020/11/09/opinion/sway-kara-swisher-esther-perel.html?, accessed December 4, 2020.